Sandy —

May you continue
to thrive in God's amazing
love for you, my friend
and sister in Christ.

Love,
Jamie Bonner
5-24-18

THRIVING
Love IN GOD'S

SEVEN POWERFUL STEPS TO HEAL
BODY, SOUL, AND SPIRIT AFTER
BREAST CANCER

SUZANNE BONNER, M.S.Eᴅ.

WESTBOW
PRESS®
A DIVISION OF THOMAS NELSON
& ZONDERVAN

WestBow Press books may be ordered through booksellers or by contacting:

WestBow Press
A Division of Thomas Nelson & Zondervan
1663 Liberty Drive
Bloomington, IN 47403
www.westbowpress.com
1 (866) 928-1240

Because of the dynamic nature of the Internet, any web addresses or links contained in this book may have changed since publication and may no longer be valid. The views expressed in this work are solely those of the author and do not necessarily reflect the views of the publisher, and the publisher hereby disclaims any responsibility for them.

Any people depicted in stock imagery provided by Thinkstock are models, and such images are being used for illustrative purposes only.
Certain stock imagery © Thinkstock.

ISBN: 978-1-9736-1334-3 (sc)
ISBN: 978-1-9736-1335-0 (hc)
ISBN: 978-1-9736-1333-6 (e)

Library of Congress Control Number: 2018900035

Print information available on the last page.

WestBow Press rev. date: 01/31/2018

This book is dedicated to every woman who
has—or has had—breast cancer.

You do not walk this path alone.

You walk with a group of "sisters," bonded forever by our
disease. Together we learn how to heal by sharing helpful stories
about our own walks, including the strengths we discovered
in the battle, and the hope we've found along the way.

This is my story of my walk with breast cancer, dear sisters.
May God use it to bless each of you with His complete healing
in your whole person: body, soul, and spirit.

CONTENTS

I will tell of the Lord's unfailing love.
I will praise the Lord for all He has done.
Isaiah 63:7 (NLT)

Three things will last forever—faith, hope, and love—and
the greatest of these is love. 1 Corinthians 13:13 (NLT)

DISCLAIMER

This book wasn't written to give you advice about medical treatment. I'm not a medically trained health-care professional. Nothing in this book is intended in any way to substitute for medical advice, treatment, or testing; or to encourage you to forego being under a doctor's care for all medical treatment.

This book simply shares my story of healing, and what I learned along the way. As part of that, I will include the treatment options I chose. I also want you to know that I am blessed to know and walk with many other women who chose different treatment options. They, too, are alive today.

I cannot promise you a set number of years of life, dear sisters. Only God knows the length of your days. What I can do is help you live your life in the way God created for you to live, and offer you His Biblical promise of living with Him forever in Heaven when you acknowledge and accept Him as your Lord and Savior.

ACKNOWLEDGMENTS

A special thank you to Al, Sam, and Andy for encouraging
my walk with women with cancer and the writing of this book.

And to all the sisters and friends who have walked this journey
with me, I offer my sincere thanks for all you've shared
with me. Individual names are too numerous to mention
without the risk of leaving someone out accidentally.

Please know I love each of you.

INTRODUCTION

Breast cancer is more than a physical disease, dear sisters. It is also an emotional and spiritual disease affecting every part of ourselves: body, soul, and spirit. I sensed this personally seventeen years ago when I was diagnosed with breast cancer. Later, after walking with many other sisters who also had breast cancer, I have a better understanding of how we can more fully heal and begin to thrive in ways we'd forgotten were possible.

Thriving is far more than surviving the disease, dear sisters. Statistics tell us there is a 90% survival rate of five years for all women with breast cancer, and as high as 99% for women with cancer found only in the breast (cancer.net). Almost all of us will survive, but I want you to know we can also **Thrive**.

God always intended for us to **Thrive**, dear sisters. How do we know this? His Word tells us so:

> (Growing in grace) they will still **thrive** and bear fruit and prosper in old age. They will flourish and be vital and fresh (rich in trust and love and contentment); Psalm 92:14 (AMP)

We can flourish, dear sisters. There is even a word for this, **Shalom**, and it is a word of blessing. It is the way Jesus greeted or said good-bye to people when He lived on earth. He wanted His **Shalom** for everyone: a blessing of His grace, His mercy, and His love, freely given to sustain each of us through the trials of life. Peace would be the result; many translators stop with this single word of blessing, but

Jesus did not. Jewish dictionaries tell us the Shalom blessing from Jesus also included *wholeness and completeness* for each of us.

Isn't that what we all want in our lives, dear sisters, perhaps most noticeably when we have cancer? We want a peace that we can count on; a Shalom blessing, if you will. And we want wholeness and completeness in all parts of ourselves: body, soul, and spirit.

God wants us to know that with His help, we can use this cancer to create a richer, more complete life for ourselves. Together we can heal our wounds—physically, spiritually, and emotionally—by addressing all possible causes of cancer within ourselves.

But we cannot do it alone.

Dear sisters, to fully thrive and prevent a reoccurrence, we cannot stop healing when the cancerous tumors are removed. We must also be willing, with God's help, to look at our lives more deeply, and discover what other parts of ourselves need to be healed.

This book gives you seven powerful steps to take in addition to your medical treatment. These seven steps will walk you through a process of more fully healing your complete self: body, soul, and spirit. This process is a walk, not a race. This healing is best found, my dear sisters, by taking the time to become wholly, completely well, one step at a time.

May His Shalom be with you always!

A BREAST CANCER DIAGNOSIS

It was the Friday before Labor Day. Sam, our oldest son, and Andy, our younger son, were still in school. We were going to one of those hotels with a water park in Phoenix for the holiday weekend. Reservations were made; bags were packed. We were just waiting for the kids to be done for the day, so we could leave early the next morning.

Two weeks before, I'd had a breast ultrasound for a lump I'd felt under my arm near my left breast. I'd watched it through one full menstrual cycle. When it didn't go away,

I asked my nurse practitioner if she would schedule me for an ultrasound. Mammograms didn't work for me, as I had dense breast tissue.

During the ultrasound visit, the surgeon drained the cyst. Then he said, "The good news is the cyst you were feeling is benign. But there is a dark shadow underneath it that I want to check out. It's probably nothing. But since your kids are so young, I want to be sure. It's a rather large area, so let's get you scheduled for outpatient surgery so I can take a better look."

Within a week, I had the outpatient surgery. I requested light sedation and when it was over, I woke up quickly. For some reason, I asked one of the nurses if I could see what they removed from my breast.

"That's the size of a matchbox car!" I exclaimed, as only the mom of two young boys would. I was curious why the doctor removed so much tissue, but figured he was just being cautious.

When the week passed with no word on the results, I was anxious to know everything was fine. I finally called the doctor's office, hoping to catch them before they left for the holiday weekend. The nurse came to the phone when I told the receptionist why I was calling.

When I heard the words: "How soon can you be here?" I knew the news wasn't good. Every woman knows when it's good news, someone at the office says: "Everything is clear. No need to come in. Be sure and have an exam again next year."

I hung up the phone after saying we'd be right in, and sank to the steps with a guttural wail that comes from knowing something is terribly wrong. I wanted the nurse to say what every woman wants to hear after a test: "I'm so sorry. We must have forgotten to call. That dark shadow under the cyst was just normal breast tissue. Have a wonderful Labor Day weekend. Nothing to worry about."

But that is not what I heard.

I wailed and wailed. How else could I describe the hopeless sound that came from some lost canyon deep inside me?

My husband, Alan, came running in the house, now frantic himself. "What's wrong? Did something happen to the kids? What?"

"The doctor's office wants to see me right away. It's not good news," I replied.

When we arrived, the doctor and his assistant were very sad looking, and as shocked as we were. In the year 2000, a woman in her early forties who appears to be healthy was very unlikely to have cancer of any kind, let alone at least a dozen or more cancerous tumors in her breast!

The doctor sent the rest of the staff home, I guess, as the office got very quiet. We had his full attention. He just sat with us in that space of shock and churning emotions, allowing us to ask questions, make comments, whatever we needed to do.

Having not been through this before, I had no script, no "OK, this is what we need to know now." Instead, I just had this diagnosis I wanted to send back, and get on with the weekend!

When we asked what comes next, the doctor compassionately went over my options, suggesting we think about my choices over the weekend—as if we could think about anything else—and come back early next week to let him know what we decided.

Leaving there, I thought angrily: "I just don't have time for this. This can't be happening! We are new in town, we have two young boys, and no family anywhere close by. This has to be wrong!"

But my gut told me the report was correct, and we would just have to deal with this. Fear, on the other hand, told me I was going to die. If I had twelve tumors in a small part of my breast, how many were in the whole breast? "It's terminal, and you will die," my mind screamed repeatedly.

I worked hard to keep my feelings inside. We needed to get the boys from a neighbor who kindly picked them up from their schools, and get home. It wouldn't help for my husband to feel my hysteria, too, in front of the boys.

When we got home, Alan did what people were just beginning to do back then; he looked for information online. Alan is a doer, and this gave him something concrete to do. I think I went into my "kids home from school routine," which was comforting for me. I got them some snacks, talking a bit about the water park we were going to and how much fun we'd have, while struggling to act as normal as possible.

It was a good diversion for both of us. Otherwise, I might have screamed: "Your mother has breast cancer, and she's going to die, and who will raise you kids?" at our four and six- year-old sons. Hysteria none of us needed, even though feelings of panic were racing around inside me.

Because I was interested in alternative medicine, Al looked for places I could go for "treatments" that might prevent me from having more surgery, or risk what he feared the most: that a surgeon would cut through more tumors and the cancer would spread everywhere, like some uncontrollable force. He seemed to vacillate between gathering information and being in total denial.

My reaction was just the opposite. If a doctor could remove the entire breast, and just "get rid of the cancer," I thought that would be the best fix. Just cut it off and get that cancer out of me!

Various options would be presented over the next few weeks, but before we left for the water park the next day, Al had found a place online called "Oasis of Hope," and requested information. It gave us a feeling of being proactive, since both of us default to our "do something to fix this or make it go away" personalities under stress.

When I first looked at the website for "Oasis of Hope,"
I felt like God was giving me a sign about this place. My
husband was not a believer, yet he recommended a hospital
that proclaimed on its website: "Jesus is the Master
Physician."

That got my attention! Maybe I needed to put my trust
in more than just my doctors, or "cures" I found on my own.
Cancer certainly wasn't something I could fix alone!

FACING THE DIAGNOSIS

On the Tuesday morning following our weekend trip, the boys returned to school, and I was left to deal with my diagnosis. Alan and I returned to my surgeon to make decisions about my options for treatment (another lumpectomy or a mastectomy). I took along a notebook, so I could write things down. (Sisters, I highly recommend you do this, too. Now is a great time to get a notebook or Journal for yourself, if you don't already have one. You'll be using it throughout this book and at your appointments. I also recommend you have someone with you at all your appointments for another set of ears.)

When we left the surgeon's office, Al and I had a better idea of our next steps. A flurry of appointment scheduling began with unfamiliar and frightening types of doctors: an oncologist, a radiologist, and a plastic surgeon. I also had appointments at a prosthesis place, a lab for additional bloodwork, and with radiology for yet another mammogram to confirm that cancerous tumors were still present in my left breast.

Scheduling and appointments required most of my attention when the boys were at school. When they were home, they needed Mom to be her usual self, and keep their lives on a regular, even keel. I sensed my husband also needed that. Although I'd lived my whole life burying my feelings inside myself to try to maintain peace and harmony, I now found this very difficult to do with a cancer diagnosis.

In desperation, I picked up the notebook I'd taken to this last appointment with the doctor, and started writing down my thoughts and feelings about everything happening in my life. I'd journaled sporadically before, but something about the seriousness of having breast cancer made it essential that I start again right now.

JOURNALING TO HELP YOU HEAL

I found journaling to be a great way to think things through on paper about my diagnosis and treatment. Journaling helped my mind focus, and it allowed me to vent my thoughts and feelings about this cancer privately. (I could decide later if I wanted to express them to another person.) There is something about expressing your feelings without censorship that helps you get a better perspective, sweet sister. I believe it's also very healing to our souls.

I began to write about the uncomfortable feelings bubbling up inside me that I could no longer suppress. As I wrote about them, they would sometimes surface so strongly that I had to scream into pillows, or even beat the bed in fury. I often used a metal cane to do this, pounding with enough force to be able to get my intense anger out.

Thankfully, this idea of beating the bed had come back to me from my graduate training in school counseling. I'd learned that it's much healthier to release emotions through journaling, or by talking to a neutral, trained counselor or therapist, or by hitting a punching bag or pillow instead of harming anyone, including ourselves.

Dear sisters, as I journaled daily and pounded frequently, I began to sense that my many tumors were buried hurts and losses I had repressed and never resolved with anyone, including God. As I worked through these feelings, I could identify what I thought was buried in each tumor.

Unusual, I know, but it seemed to work for me. I just wanted those unresolved, buried hurts out of me—just like the cancer! It was probably the only thing that gave me the courage to dissect those ugly globs inside me; to literally pop them open like an infected pimple or boil, letting all the gunk come pouring out.

Much to my surprise, I learned that "getting it all out" is very healing. I also learned that God does not want us to keep our feelings buried inside us. He wants us to bring all of them to Him for healing. In 1 Peter 5:7, His Word tells to "give all your worries and cares to God, for He cares about you."

I didn't have to ignore or minimize my feelings anymore! This was both freeing and frightening news to me, but something I was determined to do. I didn't want the cancer to return!

My buried toxic emotions may not have been an actual cancer, dear sisters, but they certainly were a "toxic growth" that kept me from emotionally healing, perhaps making me more susceptible to a reoccurrence in the future.

Dear sisters, pull out your Journal or notebook, and take some time to write down any thoughts or feelings that came up for you when you read this. Perhaps you felt anger, fear, confusion, intrigue, or something else entirely. By writing out whatever you are feeling, you will gain clarity and go deeper into what could be the emotional root of your cancer.

***

If you are new to journaling, you can begin by asking God to join you in your quiet time with Him. This is the type of prayer I use most often. It becomes a personal conversation with God where I talk to Him as my trusted advisor, as well as my Lord and Savior, and I listen for His answers. I have found this approach quiets my mind, and allows me to write down my thoughts, feelings, worries, concerns, joys, and praise—anything that's on my mind or in my heart that day.

When I finish, I ask God for His thoughts and wisdom on whatever I'm feeling or going through. Then I open my Bible to the pages He gives me. (I simply hold my Bible in my hands. With my eyes still closed, I turn it around several times and randomly open it, expecting His answer or comments to be somewhere on those two pages.)

As I read His Word on these pages, asking only for His insights and understanding, dear sisters, I believe I truly hear from God. The Bible is God's Word, and it stands for all eternity. It is powerfully infused with His Truth, and it does not return to Him void:

> So will My word be which goes out of My mouth: It will not return to Me void (useless, without result), without accomplishing what I desire, and without succeeding in the matter for which I sent it. Isaiah 55:11 (AMP)

When we ask God for His wisdom from His Word, He always provides it for us, but we must do our part. We must spend time reading the Bible to discover the wisdom in His Word. Then, we must commit to walking out His wisdom in faith by acting on what He has revealed to us through His Word.

> If you need wisdom, ask our generous God, and He will give it to you. He will not rebuke you for asking. But when you ask Him, be sure that your faith is in God alone. Do not waver, for a person with divided loyalty is as unsettled as a wave of the sea that is blown and tossed by the wind. James 1:5-6

Sweet sisters, you can really trust God to answer you by offering insight and healing for whatever is going on in your life. His Word tells us so!

As you begin to journal, I encourage you to be honest in your writing. It is for your eyes only. God knows how you feel anyway, so you are not going to shock or offend Him, or lose His love, no matter what you say. It really is okay to let it all out here. It is also very healing if you will commit to the daily habit of journaling.

JOURNALING, SEVENTEEN YEARS LATER

Seventeen years later, dear sisters, I still find journaling essential to my well-being.

Soon after I wake up, I pour a glass of tea and sit in "my chair."

I pick up my Journal and pen from the table close by, and write out what's on my mind. Some days it's heavier, other days it's lighter, and sometimes it's about a dream or something that happened the day before. If nothing is bubbling around in me that morning, I'll simply open my Bible and write about what God gives me that day.

After years of burying my feelings in my body, which I still strongly sense contributed to my tumors, I now literally fear keeping negative (or even happy) feelings buried inside me. It is the buried part that bothers me. It usually means I am suppressing my emotions rather than experiencing them or choosing to express them before letting them go.

I am still brutally honest in my Journal, certain that God already knows what I am thinking, feeling, or wanting to do. I've learned that only He can shed a new light on, or lovingly listen to, my true feelings.

I now know that He will never hold it against me or condemn me for any of my feelings; and He always offers insight and suggestions through His Word, a devotional, or from a friend. God is faithful and truly wants to see us through this difficult time, sweet sister!

His Word tells us:

> Therefore there is no condemnation (no guilty verdict, no punishment) for those who belong to Christ Jesus (who believe in Him as their personal Lord and Savior). Romans 8:1 (AMP)

I have also learned to take my feelings to the Lord first. Sometimes it's enough to express them to Him through my prayers and journaling. At other times, He gives me the words to express myself to someone, if that's what I need to do. Running my feelings through Him first is a form of discipline that isn't always easy, but it keeps me from making a mess of a relationship or circumstance by reacting too quickly.

If strong feelings come up for me, words are often hard to find. Drawing or making a collage helps. By creating a representation of how I feel, I can move beyond a more analytical form of writing. This can be helpful to you, too, if you feel stuck writing. If a word or words come to you as you draw or color, just jot them down on the paper somewhere. Experiment with this, and see what works best for you.

I've heard the suggestion that writing two or three handwritten pages every morning is a helpful approach. When I do this, even informally, I notice at first there is a lot of "dumping" of a variety of emotions. Soon little nuggets of insight or direction emerge as I keep writing. And I always feel more peaceful when I'm done, especially if I've taken the time to ask God what He thinks through His Word.

There is no obligation to write a certain number of words or pages each day, dear sisters. If you are processing through a lot of feelings and have the time, you will usually write more. Other times, you'll write less, or record just a few words. Use your journaling time primarily to connect with yourself, and with God. This will help you heal, I promise.

GRATITUDE JOURNAL

Several years ago, while going through another difficult time of depression, I decided to add another "notebook" to my journaling process. I call this my Gratitude Journal, and I open this Journal first every morning. I simply (although not always easily) write down seven things I'm grateful for. Sometimes it's something stellar; sometimes it's simply that I got up, or I have tea to drink, or the dog is fine. (Some days, I do grasp for gratefulness, dear sisters, so I start by noticing the little comforts I take for granted.)

The last item is always a thank you for God: "He is my Savior," or "He is with me," or "He is the King of Kings," or for an answer to prayer.

Listing seven things each day is significant enough to make me really think about what I am grateful for. It's another discipline that helps transform my mind into healing thoughts about God, rather than troubles, or fears, or things of the world. (Those go in my "get-it-all-out" Journal.)

When you feel ready, I encourage you to begin your own gratitude

Journal. It is a choice you can make to become more aware of the good—large or small—that is also happening in your life.

NOW WHAT DO I DO?

After surgery and treatment, I was ready to heal and become a "new and improved" (healthier!) version of myself who would be cancer-free the rest of my life. I believed if I "got cancer" once, I certainly could "get it" again! My body obviously knew how to grow cancerous tumors, having produced at least a dozen of them at one time!

Like you, I did not want to repeat this cancer experience again!

Although my medical team had done their job well and with great compassion, I was discharged with just a "come back for a check-up in three months, or sooner if I felt another lump." I needed more!

I had so many unanswered questions racing through my mind:

- Why me? Why did I get cancer? Heart disease runs rampant in the women on both sides of my family, not breast cancer!
- How do I keep the cancer from coming back? Prevention seemed far better to me than relying on early detection, although that's important, too.
- How do I put my life back together when I feel raw emotionally, and so vulnerable to the cancer returning?
- What about all these emotions I'm feeling that I don't know how to deal with?
- What really happens to me when I die? Will I go to Heaven? How do I know Heaven exists?
- Is this cancer a punishment from God?
- Who will help me now that I won't be seeing my medical team very often?

I wanted someone "in charge" of my healing who would walk with me through those uncertain early days, dear sisters. I wanted someone to give me a handout full of next steps telling me how to move past the *surviving* mode. I even dared to hope I could do more than just survive. I wanted to **thrive** like I did many years ago before life became painful and stressful.

Much to my disappointment, I found out there was no handout. I wasn't assigned a cancer wellness coach, nor was I ever promised that my life could be better, even though I was now cancer-free. No one seemed to know exactly what I should begin doing after treatment to prevent this cancer from reoccurring.

I discovered I had to take responsibility for my own health and well-being. I needed to be proactive because I believed my life literally depended on how I walked out the healing from whatever was causing these cancerous tumors to grow. Was it the food I was eating? Toxins in the environment? Or could it be the stress in my life, or the emotional toll buried hurts and turmoil were taking on me? Was the cause unexpressed grief or anger? Or was it a lack of spiritual connection and meaning in my life?

Or was it all of those? I didn't know, but I had two young sons to raise. I had a strong reason for living many more years!

I decided to learn all I could about healing after cancer, and what it meant to have true wellness for *all of me*: body, soul, and spirit. I learned that wellness, or wholeness, is what God intends for us, dear sisters, but we must do our part. Only we can do the hard work of walking out our own healing, one step at a time. This is what I call the cancer walk.

I found I had to choose to make some changes—even the hard ones—so I could be well. I had to dig deep, and uncover painful and "life-stealing" behaviors and emotions. I had to learn what a healthier way of life in body, soul, and spirit would look like, and how I could achieve this in my own life.

At the same time, I wanted to know where I would spend eternity if I died. Cancer made me realize I wasn't going to live forever, no matter what I did. I didn't know how this cancer walk was going to play out. I only knew I was finally going to be willing to ask for help, and listen to what others shared with me. That was enough for now as I "suited up" for the walk.

Dear sisters, I want you to know that you also have choices. You, too, have the right to take time to care for yourself, and to do what is necessary for your own healing. As a child of God, you have the right to know you are so *worth it* in His eyes. God wants you to know He created you to see your extraordinary value to Him through His loving eyes, calling you the very "apple of His eye" in Zechariah 2:8 (AMP).

I also want you to know that there is a way to turn this cancer experience into one of blessing, healing, and abundant life that God intends for each of us!

THE WALK

Sweet sisters, life after breast cancer—*the Walk*—can only be done one step at a time. Although I wanted the new, healthier me right after the mastectomy, I felt and looked like anything but a new, healthier version of myself! You understand what I'm saying, I'm sure.

As I began to walk out my own healing, **seven distinct steps** began to take shape in the following order. I've written them as questions you can ask yourself, knowing that these same questions have helped me—and many other sisters—heal:

- **Faith**: Who or what do you believe in? Where will you put your trust?
- **Feelings**: What emotions are you feeling about your breast cancer diagnosis?
- **Family**: How do you define family?
- **Forgiveness**: Are you carrying around anger, resentment, or bitterness towards someone for something?
- **Food**: How do you view food? Do you think it can make a difference in your healing now, and help you prevent a cancer reoccurrence later?
- **Fitness**: What do you do for exercise most days? Are you willing to become more active when you are able?
- **Fun**: What brings you joy and laughter that doesn't hurt someone else?

We'll begin with the first step, **Faith**, in the larger section called "**Healing Your Spirit.**" My own spirit felt shredded, damaged, and nearly destroyed at this point in my life, dear sisters. Although I'd made changes in my diet right away to help keep the cancer from spreading (see F5: Food), my spirit is what needed immediate attention for complete healing to even be possible.

PART 1

Healing Your Spirit

Your spirit is your life force; your spirit is what gives you life.

And the Lord God formed man of the dust of the ground,
and breathed into His nostrils the breath of life …
—Genesis 2:7 (KJV)

Your spirit is the part of you that is eternal.

For then dust will return to the earth, and the
spirit will return to God who gave it.
—Ecclesiastes 12:7 (NLT)

Without a spirit, the body is dead.

You take away their spirit,
they expire and return to the dust.
—Psalm 104:29 (NASB)

F1: FAITH

Rebecca, a neighbor I carpooled with, agreed to pick up the boys while we were at the surgeon's office getting the diagnosis. She had a friend, Phyllis, who was a cancer survivor with an impactful story. When we returned from the doctor's office, Rebecca asked me if Phyllis could stop by later and share her cancer story with me. Rebecca thought it would be very encouraging.

Here's what Phyllis told me within hours of my diagnosis:

> *When my kids were young and still at home, I was diagnosed with lymphoma. The cancer had already spread all over my body. After completing the usual rounds of chemotherapy locally, the only medical option remaining was a bone marrow transplant.*
>
> *At this point in my life, I went to church, but I wasn't what I would call strong in my faith. It's something I did; it was the way I was raised.*
>
> *However, when I had my diagnosis "of no hope," I turned to God in desperation. I prayed, "Lord, if You will let me live to raise my children, I will give my life to You."*
>
> *I went on to have the bone marrow transplant at a hospital located four hours from home, in total isolation other than hospital workers in hazmat suits.*
>
> *When the treatments were done, I was told by the hospital staff:*
>
> *"I'm sorry, but your bone marrow transplant didn't work so we are dismissing you from the hospital to go home*

1

and live out your remaining days. There is nothing else we can do, and we need the bed for another patient awaiting a transplant."

Just like that, I was sent home to die, with no compassion expressed, and no hope offered. I was shocked by the way I was suddenly treated. Many of the medical staff I'd dealt with before had been very compassionate and professional, but now I felt abruptly dismissed because their treatment had failed. Right then I made the decision to continue to pray and trust in God instead of the staff's predictions for me.

And you know what? The cancer staff was wrong! I am alive today, ten years later! I've been cancer free ever since I turned to the only Hope I had left, and put my faith in God.

Dear sisters, Phyllis is alive and well today, twenty-seven years later!

I will always be grateful that Phyllis took the time to share her story of hope with me during my darkest moments right after the diagnosis. Her story showed me the power of stepping out in faith, regardless of how weak my faith might be.

She also showed me how other survivors can offer so much comfort, support, and hope to each other.

★★★

Sweet sisters, I came to realize I'd played at "faith" most of my life, never taking it too seriously. I was raised in a Bible-following Christian church and school, but I never really had much of a personal relationship with God. I believed in Him, but I wasn't sure I needed Him. And I didn't think I could get to know Him personally and intimately.

That's hard to admit, sweet sisters. *Really hard.*

Unfortunately, I'd left the Christian faith I grew up with and became what I would call a seeker dabbling in anything and everything about "spirituality" that caught my attention during a difficult time at the end of my first marriage. At first, New Age beliefs appeared to accept all forms of religion, and that felt like the best fit for me.

In my continual seeking several years before breast cancer, I'd even tried reading an atheist author, Carl Sagan, at a husband's insistence, but I couldn't last for more than a few days of trying to believe there was *no* God.

If I gave up my belief in God, then there was no hope, no heaven, and no eternal life to look forward to. If there truly was no God, what was the point of this world? What would be the meaning of life?

As a farm girl, I grew up seeing the astounding beauty and presence of God all around me. I knew there was a God, even if I saw Him as distant and judgmental. I didn't want to be done with God; I just wanted to find a loving God who would stop the series of losses I'd experienced. I wanted to find the God my grandmother had known so well. I wanted to find the God that had given her such hope-filled peace.

Thankfully, the seeds of Christian faith had been planted early in my life by my beloved grandmother. She told me she often prayed for me during her daily talks with God. Because her sight was failing, I would read to her from her Bible and hymnal. She would stroke my arm as I sat beside her in her chair, and she would talk to me about Jesus. Her faith was so real I could feel it.

I grew up in a household troubled by my other grandfather's alcoholism, so my time with her often felt like the only peaceful thing in my life when I was little. Because she lived each day with Jesus, His Spirit was very much alive in her. I felt totally accepted, loved, and okay whenever I was with her. We didn't go anywhere, and she didn't buy me anything, but she gave me the love of Jesus whenever I visited.

I needed love, not things. Somehow Grandmother knew exactly what I needed.

Of course, I didn't understand that then, but I can clearly see it now. The freely offered gift of her time and her faith would ultimately save my life in the only way that mattered, for all eternity! Grandmother must have known this too.

As I sat there beside her, she would sometimes say with such peace and joy, "I am ready to meet my Maker." She didn't say she was ready "to die," which is very meaningful to me now. She thought of death as more of a transition into eternal life, with her eyes always on the prize of living with God for all eternity because of her faith in Jesus as her Lord and Savior.

She was certain of where she was going, as if she had acquired a deep spiritual sight as she lost much of her physical sight. She never complained about her many physical challenges, or any losses, or regrets. She always had a good word to say about her God.

I am so grateful I had her in my life as a young child! God willing, I hope to do this for my future grandchildren someday.

★★★

Looking back, I believe God called me to return to Him at a time when my life was literally crumbling around me. It often seems to work that way.

Our family had recently moved across the country with our five- and seven-year-old sons. We'd barely moved into our home before I received the breast cancer diagnosis. We had no family close enough to help us, and now I had twelve "known-so-far" cancerous tumors in my left breast, right above my distressed heart.

I was stressed, dear sisters—very stressed. My heart already felt broken from the deaths of my entire birth family, including my younger brother, plus a miscarriage, a divorce, and a new diagnosis of clinical depression. I felt alone without hope and with nowhere to turn in this new community.

Questions raced through my mind. My dad had died during treatment for lung cancer—the only cancer occurrence in our family—so would I die too? And if I died, who would raise our children? Who would be their mother? I knew firsthand the huge hole in my own heart when my mother died from heart disease too early in my life, and I would do anything to spare my children that horrible feeling.

I was desperate. The cancerous tumors caused me overwhelming fear and desperation in the beginning. Yet those same lumps led me to a path of peace and salvation at the end.

How could that be?

Because in my time of desperation and great fear, I opened a Bible I'd been given about a year earlier by a man with the same first name as my brother. We'd met at an Al-Anon meeting I'd attended after my brother's death. During the meeting, I'd shared that I'd never really known a higher power or God who was loving or kind. I talked about how alcoholism had affected my life and likely took my brother's life at age thirty-eight. I admitted to the group that I only knew a God of losses, not love. I thought all the losses in my life were punishment from God for something I'd done. Or had neglected to do.

When this kind man approached me after that Al-Anon meeting, he wanted to show me his Life Recovery Bible (NLT). When I mentioned that I'd grown up with a King James Bible (KJV), which was hard for me to understand, he offered me his own Bible. By the wear and tear and the gentle way he held it out to me, I could tell this was a much-treasured Bible.

Yet he was giving it to me, a total stranger, to help me find a loving God and some peace from the losses! I was moved beyond words, seeing his gift as perhaps he saw it—as essential to my own recovery as it was to his. We'd both been through difficult times that only God could heal, and yet he knew what I had yet to grasp: only God can heal our wounds and give us hope again.

This Bible became my lifeline of hope when I was faced with a cancer diagnosis a year later. I cried out and asked God for a sign that He would heal me, praying as Phyllis prayed: "Please let me live, dear God, so I can raise our children." Wanting to know God's answer, and seeking a confirmation I would live, I opened the Life Recovery Bible, believing He would answer me through His Word.

God used that Bible, which included a 12-step commentary on the Scriptures, to lead me to a verse of hope and promise I could cling to, even though I still wasn't fully following the Christian faith:

> And He said to her, "Daughter, your faith has made you well. Go in peace. Your suffering is over." Mark 5:34

What a powerful Scripture to hold onto and believe! I took hold of that promise and clung to it throughout my entire walk.

Join me now, sweet sisters, in reading this Scripture in its entirety. Perhaps God will give you a sense that this story is also for you.

A Woman Touches Jesus' Clothes

When Jesus had gone across by boat to the other side of the lake, a vast crowd gathered around Him on the shore.

The leader of the local synagogue, whose name was Jairus, came and fell down before Him, pleading with Him to heal his little daughter.

Jesus went with him, and the crowd thronged behind. In the crowd was a woman who had been sick for twelve years with a hemorrhage She had suffered much from many doctors through the years, and had become poor from paying them, and was no better but, in fact, was worse. She had heard all about the wonderful miracles Jesus did, and that is why she came up behind Him through the crowd and touched His clothes.

For she thought to herself, 'If I can just touch His clothing, I will be healed.' As soon as she had touched Him, the bleeding stopped, and she knew she was well!

Jesus realized at once that healing power had gone out from Him, so He turned around in the crowd and asked, "Who touched My clothes?"

His disciples said to Him, "All the crowd pressing around You, and You ask who touched You?"

But He kept on looking around to see who it was who had done it. Then the frightened woman, trembling at the realization of what had happened to her, came and fell at His feet and told Him what she had done. **And He said to her, "Daughter, your faith has made you well; go in peace, healed of your disease."**

The paralyzing fear quieted down as I began to believe I could walk out my healing with God's help and live. Maybe God did love me, and I wasn't totally alone. Maybe breast cancer wasn't a punishment after all!

Perhaps it was those seeds of faith Grandma had sown in me, along with all the Scriptures and hymns I learned as a child in a Christian school and Sunday school, that took root and began to grow again when I faced this cancer diagnosis.

Sweet sister, I don't know what, if anything, you believe in. Maybe you are in a place like I was: accepting the faith of your childhood, but never bothering to make it your own. Maybe you believe there is a God, but you don't really know Him. Or maybe you think God doesn't exist, or He doesn't love you, or He has abandoned you with this diagnosis.

Perhaps you go to church, but don't spend any time outside of church getting to know God personally. You figure you'll have plenty of time to do that in Heaven.

When I was diagnosed, the New Age beliefs I had left me feeling like I caused all my troubles because I couldn't control the bad things that were happening to me. Either I wasn't thinking the right thoughts,

ting my dreams" in the "correct" way, causing

sses I was experiencing.

ng was my fault.

at nothing from this New Age way of believing

al hope to hang onto. If it was up to me to create my

y, or if I was having so many major losses occur because of

e awful past lives I'd lived (a New Age false belief that we keep cycling through different lives until we finally get it right), then I was doomed. I wanted out of this mess!

The verse from Mark 5:34 ("Daughter, your faith has made you well; go in peace, healed of your disease.") showed me a path that fit together in a way that only God could see the design, but it gave me solid hope. This hope got me through a difficult diagnosis, treatment, and frequent fears of a reoccurrence every time I had an ache, or pain, or a lump. Perhaps you know what that's like!

This precious passage also became the foundation of walking out my healing completely: in body, soul, and spirit. I believed right then I was healed in the sense that I wouldn't die from cancer. But I also believed to be completely healed, I couldn't stop with surgery and treatment. While doing the work necessary to heal physically and make my body more cancer-resistant to prevent reoccurrences, I also needed to do the work necessary to heal emotionally and spiritually.

Dear sisters, I had to be willing to look at the whole person—body, soul, and spirit—and hold each part of me up to the light of God's Word.

I had a source of support every step of the way, if I would accept the Savior's help. And the gift of a Life Recovery Bible would soon lead me to a loving God of my understanding, by getting to know Him through His Word.

Mark 5:34 also allowed me to reject the inner voices that were screaming "I would surely die at a young age" because that is what my entire birth family did! Since my dad had died during treatment for stage IV lung cancer, cancer would probably kill me too! With thirteen tumors in my breast, surely cancer had spread throughout my body!

The scary voice in my head went on and on with fatalistic thoughts presented as truth.

They were lies! Dear sisters, fear never presents itself as God's Truth! Only God's Word speaks His Truth; fear always speaks to us with crazy lies.

Maybe you understand because fear is doing the same thing to you. I would guess, dear sister, you've had your own moments of these emotionally charged, full of fear rants in your mind, regardless of where you are in your personal cancer walk. Having walked out seventeen years from those frightful days, I will share this with you:

I found I needed a faith in something or someone greater than myself. More than this vagueness of what or who to believe in, I found I needed a faith in a God I came to know personally as my loving and kind Savior to give me a peace that would last.

I do not have to tell you that there are many things you can believe in, many "religions or paths" you can follow. I chose to believe what God told me in His Word, instead of what fear told me. Hopefully you also know that whatever you choose to believe in is completely your choice, too, dear sisters.

In God's great love for His children—which is all of us, whether we accept Him as our Savior or not—He gave us a significant gift: the free will to choose how to live our lives, and whether we choose to believe in Him or not.

This, sweet sisters, is the ultimate form of love. Perhaps you, too, have heard this old saying: "If you love something, set it free. If it comes back to you, it's yours. If it doesn't, it never was."

This isn't a Bible verse, but I believe it describes a basic human truth. We cannot hang onto anyone if he or she wants to go. (Believe me, I have tried.) We can be there if he or she decides to come back, but we really cannot make anyone stay with us. Even if they physically stay, they are already gone emotionally.

God understands this. He knows real love is a choice, not a robotic response. He wants us to be free to choose Him, or not.

Like a loving parent, who loves his or her child regardless of what the child does or doesn't do, God continues to love us all our lives.

I finally decided to stop "seeking," and love God back, even though every step wasn't easy, or straight, or clear. God was my only real hope, and so I said *"Yes"* to wherever this leap of faith took me.

I had to learn that faith is based on a relationship, not a religion. A religion is just a set of beliefs and practices, but a relationship is between two people—you and God—and it is very personal.

So, I committed, as best I could at the time, to getting to know God better. Christian friends suggested I spend time with Him each day in prayer and in His Word. By doing this, I began to more fully accept that only a relationship with God Himself, through His Son Jesus, could heal my broken spirit. I could not do it on my own.

Dear sisters, please pause now and get out your Journals. Write about what you are thinking and feeling after what you've just read. Consider these questions:

- How would you describe your faith?
- Where will you place your trust: doctors and medicine, God, your family, yourself, alternative medicine, or nowhere at all? Really give this important question some thought.

UNDERSTANDING FAITH

My online dictionary defines faith as "trust in God." Synonyms include confidence, trust, reliance, assurance, conviction, and belief. These are man's definitions. To understand faith more completely, I also looked at what the Bible has to say about faith.

WISDOM FROM THE WORD

This passage clearly explains God's definition of faith:

Now faith is the substance of things hoped for, the evidence of things not seen. Hebrews 11:1 (KJV)

I personally like this translation of the same verse from The Message (MSG) called "Faith in What We Don't See."

> The fundamental fact of existence is that this trust in God, this faith, is the firm foundation under everything that makes life worth living. It's our handle on what we can't see.

The translation from The Living Bible (TLB) is also very powerful:

> What is faith? It is the confident assurance that something we want is going to happen. It is the certainty that what we hope for is waiting for us, even though we cannot see it up ahead.

Read back over these three translations of Hebrews 11:1. Feel free to also look up this verse in your own Bible, or on your phone. When a passage isn't clear to me, I find it very helpful to read the verse in other translations. You might find this helpful too.

Now go back and look at your own description of faith recorded in your Journal.

- Is there anything you'd like to add or change?
- How does the online dictionary's definition of faith compare to the Bible's definition? And how does yours compare?
- Write out your understanding of faith again, if you've made any changes.

WALKING WITH JESUS IN FAITH

One of my favorite Bible stories about faith is found in Mark 14, and it involves Jesus' disciple, Peter, walking on water. Jesus and His disciples had just finished ministering to a large group of people gathered near where His boat had stopped. He had been healing the sick people in the crowd much of the day, and they'd become very hungry. Jesus told the disciples to bring Him whatever food anyone in the crowd had.

With only five loaves of bread and two fish, Jesus gave thanks and broke the loaves.

Then Jesus fed everyone—well over five thousand people—from this tiny amount of food handed to Him, and everyone witnessed this amazing miracle. Matthew 14:22-31 continues with the story of Peter stepping out in faith:

> Immediately after this, Jesus insisted that His disciples get back into the boat and cross to the other side of the lake, while He sent the people home. After sending them home, He went up into the hills by Himself to pray. Night fell while He was there alone.
>
> Meanwhile, the disciples were in trouble far away from land, for a strong wind had risen, and they were fighting heavy waves. About three o'clock in the morning Jesus came toward them, walking on the water. When the disciples saw Him walking on the water, they were terrified. In their fear, they cried out, "It's a ghost!"
>
> But Jesus spoke to them at once. "Don't be afraid," He said. "Take courage. I am here!"
>
> Then Peter called to Him, "Lord, if it's really You, tell me to come to You, walking on the water."
>
> "Yes, come," Jesus said.
>
> So, Peter went over the side of the boat and walked on the water toward Jesus. But when he saw the strong wind and the waves, he was terrified and began to sink. "Save me, Lord!" he shouted.
>
> Jesus immediately reached out and grabbed him …

Faith is what propelled Peter into the water, believing he could walk on water. He believed Jesus' words to him, and took that first step in faith.

When his fear caused his faith to falter, as our faith will sometimes do, Peter only had to reach out for Jesus, again in faith, believing that Jesus would save him.

And Jesus did.

That, sweet sisters, is what defines faith in action. We step out of the boat and take the next step, **trusting that God is on this walk with us**, and He will not let us drown in this dismal life experience called cancer. Even when our faith falters, and we begin to sink into the churning waters of fear, Jesus is already there if we will just reach out to Him in faith.

No matter how much we want to quickly be done with the whole cancer thing, I've learned it is more a matter of walking it out over time, perhaps for the rest of our lives. The best approach I've found focuses on making the next decision that's right for you; and when that's done—even if treatment lasts four months or four years—walk forward in faith to take the next step that seems right for you.

This sounds easy to do, but it isn't, dear sisters. Yes, I did it and so can you, but you also need to know the only way I could walk forward was with Jesus. I clung to the passage He gave me that said I was *healed*. This doesn't mean my life became perfect, nor does it mean walking out breast cancer was easy. I still had pain; I still had many feelings that were difficult to handle.

I also experienced the shocked look someone gets when he or she notices something is seriously wrong with you. Maybe your hair has fallen out, or you are weak and move slowly. I have been there.

When one of those airport terminal cart drivers stopped to ask if I needed a ride on my way to treatment in Mexico a month after my diagnosis, I felt such shock. "What!" I wanted to shout: "I am only forty-four years old, and just last month I was going down huge water slides with our sons at a water park. Of course, I don't need a ride!"

Instead, being the nice girl with cancer that I was (and you probably are too), I said: "No, thanks." But I walked on thinking: "Wow, I must really look sick, and I haven't even had surgery or treatment yet! How in the world am I going to live through this?"

The cancer diagnosis nearly knocked the life-spark out of me, and I was very scared to be going to another country away from my family for seventeen days. But I believed this was the next right step for me, so I did what I needed to do.

Like Peter, I clung to my faith and the promise from Jesus that said I was healed and "made well." I clung to His hand and kept putting one foot in front of the other. This, dear sweet sisters, is how we do this walk. We take the next step with Him because we can, and we've made the decision we will.

I bet that cart driver would have been surprised to see me six months later, walking on top of a sand dune in Death Valley National Park, feeling free and praising God! Surgeries and treatments were over, and I was cancer-free.

No ride needed now, thank you very much!

BUILDING HOPE

Have you lost hope, dear sister? A cancer diagnosis can overwhelm us with feelings of fear and hopelessness. Simply hearing the word *Cancer* produces fear in us. We all know someone who's died from cancer.

Sharing encouraging stories of hope like Phyllis's, or reading books like this one, are so important. Sisters need to hear that other sisters do survive breast cancer, and they often go on to live healthy, cancer-free lives. There is a very high survival rate for women with breast cancer—over 90%—even if the cancer has spread to the lymph nodes. This type of information gives us hope. I call this type of hope *generic hope.*

There is another kind of hope I call *solid hope*. Solid hope is a *faith-based hope* in Someone bigger than ourselves where we can safely place our confidence and trust. Solid hope is what healed me from cancer and years of damage to my spirit and soul. I placed my hope in God to do what I could not, and to walk with me through every step of this cancer journey. I began to trust my very survival to Him.

Hope in God replaced hope in a surgeon, my husband, a family member, a friend, or a drug treatment plan. Yes, all of those had their place in my healing, but God was in control, not me. He already knew what was best for me.

As believers in God, we can have confidence that our hope is based on solid, tangible evidence (a firm foundation) because it is grounded in the Word of God, and God cannot lie.

> God is not a man, so He does not lie. He is not human, so He does not change His mind. Has He ever spoken and failed to act? Has He ever promised and not carried it through? Numbers 23:19

Over time, I also learned from other believers that faith is also an action, and we must choose to act on our faith. Kathrine Lee, author of an online course called "The Ultimate Source," says it best in something she learned from Elsa, one of her trusted mentors:

- First, we must believe that God can do anything.
- Second, we must desire Him to take our worry burden upon Himself, and act right now as if God can do anything, and can answer any problem. He knows all things, and He is trustworthy.
- Third, we must clearly know what our part is: to be fully involved in our place of responsibility, such as having the treatment we choose. We must also give any anxiety we have about anything to God, and focus on Him alone. We must come from a place of gratitude, believing He is with us and loves us.

Pause now, dear sisters, and take out your Journal. Meditate first on what God says faith is.

- Write down your own personal understanding of faith, looking at the three action steps of faith you just read.
- Note where you are in your cancer journey, and how you can personally use these steps to give God your fears.

Joni Eareckson Tada says in the devotional <u>365 Day Brighteners for a Woman's Heart</u>:

"Faith is ... simply taking God at His word and taking the next step."

BLEEDING WOMAN AND FAITH

The Bleeding Woman is also a story about faith in action. In Mark 5:25-32 (also in Matthew 9:20-22), as soon as Jesus told the woman she was healed, she **knew** (believed) she was.

Does faith have a role in our healing? Yes, absolutely. I had very strong personal feelings about chemotherapy. I didn't believe it would heal me. I reasoned if I had no faith in chemotherapy, but I did have faith in having a mastectomy, I needed to go with the choice I believed in. (By doing what felt right for me–removing the left breast–the thirteenth and largest tumor was discovered for the first time!)

(A caveat, please. Before you decide chemotherapy isn't for you, please consult with your medical professionals. Search out as many options as you need to, and then select the treatment plan you have confidence in. Every woman's situation is different. Choose to do what is right for you, not to please someone else. You will know.)

Faith also overcomes fear. We, like our bleeding sister, can choose to approach Jesus in faith—despite the fear and our "uncleanness." This woman dared to risk it all by touching the fringes of His robe.

According to Jewish beliefs during Biblical times, bleeding women were ceremonially unclean, and anyone they touched or who touched them was also rendered ceremonially unclean. This means that bleeding women were basically shamed: isolated and shunned from having any physical contact with others. (We delve into this more under F2: Feelings.)

And yet our bleeding sister had the audacity—the bold faith—to reach out and touch the Holy Man, Jesus, and risk it all—her very life and her salvation—to the only One who could heal her.

This would have been the fear she felt when she touched Jesus in her "unclean" condition. Only sheer desperation would drive her to make such a bold move, knowing Jesus was her only remaining hope.

My dearest sisters, I, too, felt "unclean." My mistakes and my choices, including my decision not to walk with God for part of my life, caused me to feel unworthy to even ask Jesus to heal me. Yet, like the Bleeding Woman, Jesus was my only hope of complete healing.

Would you, dear sister, also like to reach out to Jesus for complete healing? Be bold and ask Jesus to heal you completely—body, soul, and spirit—with this prayer:

> *Oh, Holy Father, I come before You in the name of Jesus, and ask You to heal me completely in body, soul, and spirit. Remove this cancer that has filled my whole self with disease, and wash me clean again. Only You have the power to heal me wholly, Lord, and I trust in You to see me through anything that is ahead of me. Thank You for saving me, Lord Jesus, and securing a place for me with You in Heaven for all eternity. You are my Lord and Savior! Please give me Your peace, Your Shalom, as I face the days ahead. Amen.*

★★★

Part of my journey of faith was coming to know a God I could trust. This also meant looking at my personal idea of God as a punishing God. Did this idea have any basis in Scripture? Dear sisters, I came to understand that breast cancer is not a punishment for anyone. It is part of the fallen world we live in where painful things happen to everyone.

Through breast cancer, I learned God, in His love for us, can use anything in our life for our good, even the very things that cause us problems, pain, and hurt. I remember memorizing this verse as an elementary school student. I really didn't understand it fully then, but it has remained secure in my heart throughout my life:

> And we know that God causes everything to work together for the good of those who love God and are called according to His purpose for them. Romans 8:28

God used breast cancer to call me back to Himself, and He also helped me use breast cancer to wholly heal in body, soul, and spirit by coming to know Him as a loving God. This knowledge allowed me to have the courage to build a "new" life based on God's love for me.

I made this part of the journey like all the others, one step at a time. I wasn't always sure I was on the right path, but I just kept showing up for God: every morning during my quiet time with Him; by going to church and attending Bible studies; by having Christian women for friends; and by taking two powerful Christian classes: the previously mentioned The Ultimate Source (https://ultimatesource.tv) with Kathrine Lee, and Holly DelHousaye's SoulWork: Pilates for the Soul (Soulwork.org), taught locally by Kim Vallen. (More information on both under Resources.)

This inner work on the spirit and the soul helped me heal old religious wounds and to begin to know God as a loving God. Both were important parts of my complete healing.

Before we go further into the very essence of who God is, pause now and reflect in your personal Journal:

- How do you see God?
- Do you see Him as loving or punishing; aloof or always with you; or in some other way? Dig deep here, sweet sisters, and write out your thoughts about the very nature of God. This will help you prepare to join me as we look at how we can— with God's amazing help—heal our souls.

PART 2

Healing Your Soul

The soul is what makes us uniquely, humanly ourselves.

"…and man became a living soul." Genesis 2:7 (KJV)

The soul has three parts: mind, will, and emotions.

"Beloved, I pray that you may prosper in all things and be in health, just as your soul prospers." 3 John 1:2 (NKJV)

F2: FEELINGS

Dear sisters, even though my spirit was finally on the right path for healing, my mind and my emotions still felt full of dis-ease. I thought I was coming unglued from all the strong feelings bubbling up inside me!

- What feelings came up for you when you first heard your diagnosis? Note these in your Journal now.

I've learned women who get breast cancer tend to ignore or hide our feelings of fear, and most of our other feelings as well. We do this because we are more focused on how others feel instead of how we feel, even subconsciously preferring to take on someone else's feelings rather than our own.

And that can make us sick!

Since I often had no clue how I felt about something until others expressed their feelings, I found it helpful to learn to look more closely at what I was really feeling. Later, as I began walking with others on their own journeys through cancer, I found they, too, felt many of the same feelings I'd felt. As you read through some of the most common feelings sisters experience, be sure to add others you are experiencing too.

FEAR AND WORRY

When I first heard that I had breast cancer, I remember saying: "Breast cancer—what? You must be wrong! I'm too young! No family history! How in the world could I even get breast cancer? The report must be wrong!"

"No," my doctor said. And I barely heard the rest: He'd already gone over everything with the Pathologist. I had breast cancer. A dozen tumors so far, the doctor said once again. He knew parts of some of the tumors were still there. The biopsy turned unplanned lumpectomy did not produce clean margins. In fact, tumors were sliced through, releasing rogue cancer cells into my body.

This didn't sound good! Barely tapping down sheer terror, I walked to the car with his words buzzing around in my head. I don't think I'd ever felt so afraid for my own life before hearing the words: "You have cancer!"

I'm sure you know the feeling, dear sister. It's a tough place to be, but it's also a very natural emotional reaction.

Because fear is such an overwhelming emotion, our minds cannot stay in the paralyzing state it imposes on us. The mind will always default to fear's sidekick emotion—worry—instead. Worry gives our "freaking out" minds the belief we are dealing with the fear, unhealthy as that sounds.

Unless we interrupt that cycle, the strong emotions of fear and worry will continue to feed on each other. How then can we interrupt the cycle? Faith, the first F, helped me the most. With a foundation of faith—whether it's a new, fledgling faith, or a stronger, mature faith—we're able to get a grip on these strong, out of control emotions.

I didn't know this before my walk, dear sisters. Did you? Pause now and take out your Journal.

- Write about what fear physically feels like to you. Give yourself time to get in touch with your feelings. You are so worth it!
- Describe how you're able to deal with any feelings of fear you have. Do you have a faith in Someone greater than yourself to help you deal with your fear? Or are you still searching for something or someone to cling to?

WISDOM FROM THE WORD

What is the Bible's answer for fear?

There are many. This is one of the first verses I memorized to help me deal with my fear:

> Don't worry about anything; instead, pray about everything; tell God your needs, and don't forget to thank Him for His answers. If you do this, you will experience God's peace, which is far more wonderful than the human mind can understand. His peace will keep your thoughts and your hearts quiet and at rest as you trust in Christ Jesus. Philippians 4:6-7 (TLB)

Apostle Paul continues in verses eight and nine by suggesting we go one step further and replace our fearful thoughts with more pleasant, reassuring thoughts:

> And now, brothers, as I close this letter, let me say this one more thing: Fix your thoughts on what is true and good and right. Think about things that are pure and lovely, and dwell on the fine, good things in others. Think about all you can praise God for and be glad about. Keep putting into practice all you learned from me and saw me doing, and the God of peace will be with you.

You may be more familiar with this version, which includes verses four through seven:

> Rejoice in the Lord always. I will say it again: Rejoice! Let your gentleness be evident to all. The Lord is near. Do not be anxious about anything, but in every situation, by prayer and petition, with thanksgiving, present your requests to God. And the peace of God, which

transcends all understanding, will guard your hearts
and your minds in Christ Jesus. (NIV)

Jesus' disciple, John, gives us God's perfect antidote to fear in 1
John 4:18. For a deeper understanding, read several translations slowly
and carefully:

> Such love has no fear, because perfect love expels all
> fear. If we are afraid, it is for fear of punishment, and
> this shows that we have not fully experienced His
> perfect love. (NLT)

> There is no fear in love; but perfect love casteth out
> fear, because fear hath torment. He that feareth is not
> made perfect in love. (KJ21)

> God is love. When we take up permanent residence
> in a life of love, we live in God and God lives in us.
> This way, love has the run of the house, becomes at
> home and mature in us, so that we're free of worry on
> Judgment Day—our standing in the world is identical
> with Christ's. There is no room in love for fear. Well-
> formed love banishes fear. Since fear is crippling, a
> fearful life—fear of death, fear of judgment—is one not
> yet fully formed in love. Verses 17-18 (MSG)

Peter, another of Jesus' disciples, advises us to:

> Give all your worries and cares to God, for He cares
> about you. 1 Peter 5:7

After we've surrendered (given) our fears to God instead of trying
to fix them ourselves, the Bible assures us:

> In peace I will lie down and sleep, for You alone, O
> Lord, will keep me safe. Psalm 4:8

- Do you have your own personal Scriptures you cling to whenever you feel fear, worry, or anxiety? Pause now and record them in your Journal. Consider writing them in the front of your Journal or on an index card so you can keep them close to your heart.

ANGER

Another common emotion we sisters share is anger. While anger directed at the cancer can motivate us to make changes in our lives that help us heal, I've found that anger is often a cover-up for fear.

Anger isn't a conscious choice a fearful person makes; it is a protective reaction when we feel too vulnerable. We lash out in anger, hoping to make our fear go away. Fear makes us feel weak, but anger makes us feel powerful.

While we may feel weak in our fear and powerful in our anger, neither approach leads to long-term healing. Yes, it is okay to feel afraid. It is also okay to feel angry. What is not okay is getting mired down in either of these feelings.

Anger is a very natural emotion, but many women have been taught it's not "lady-like" to be angry, so we learn to stuff our anger. This can lead to depression, which I've heard described as "anger turned inward." It is far better to give yourself permission to feel your anger by finding nonviolent ways to express it.

This does not include yelling at others or blaming someone for "causing your cancer." No one caused it. Life caused it. Blame doesn't get you anywhere, and it certainly does not help you heal from cancer.

Nonviolent ways to express your anger besides punching pillows (not people), include running it out, screaming in the car or shower when you are alone, chopping wood, or throwing balls at a wall. You can also write it out and shred or burn the pages as we discussed under Journaling.

I was so surprised when years of buried anger erupted inside me after treatment. For too long, I had considered anger to be an unacceptable emotion for me to express; I feared losing whatever bits of love someone had for me.

I was left faced with a choice I tried to ignore: deal with the anger and whatever might be underneath it, or risk getting cancer again and dying. The choice felt that clear to me.

When I began to write out my anger, in all its fury, and taking it out on a pillow or the bed, or by screaming it out in the shower when I was home alone, I discovered that I began to feel better. It was healing to get it out!

It took weeks, even months, to unload all that anger, dear sisters!

Day after day, I beat the bed in anger, using a metal cane to try and pound out my fury. I was angry over so many things, and at so many people. Some were obvious, like the alcoholics I'd grown up with who were now dead; and some felt shameful to admit: God and my parents.

Others were buried deep within me because they felt too painful to uncover and look at: primarily the anger at myself for never being "good" enough to change others or make them love me the way I wanted to be loved.

It took a lot of pounding to tear open the rock-hard protection I had fashioned over my suppressed anger. This concrete shell had allowed me to be able to smile and appear cheerful for much of my life before cancer.

If I were to rate the intensity of my anger on a scale of zero to one hundred, I'd say it hit "one hundred" most days! Before the cancer walk began, I would have said I had very little anger bottled up inside me. I think I would have been "dead" wrong, and I believe my tumors reflected this.

Learning how to express our anger in healthier ways—and to not bottle it up or go around screaming at everyone—leads to a "dis-ease preventing" way to live, sweet sisters.

- Take some time now to think about how comfortable you are acknowledging your own anger. Write more about this in your Journal.
- Ask yourself: Is there someone or something I'm angry about that I haven't let go of? Journaling is a private way to begin uncovering buried anger that can lead to dis-ease for you.

WISDOM FROM THE WORD

If Jesus were sitting here with us, what do you think He would say about our anger? His Word tells us:

> Do not be not quick in your spirit to be angry, for irritation settles in the bosom of fools. Ecclesiastes 7:9 (MEV)

Interesting word choice, dear sisters, since "bosom" is an old-fashioned word for breast!

> A hot-tempered person stirs up conflict, but the one who is patient calms a quarrel. Proverbs 15:18 (NIV)

> In your anger do not sin: Do not let the sun go down while you are still angry, and do not give the devil a foothold. Ephesians 4:26-27 (NIV)

I believe God is telling us that buried, unresolved anger can lead to things that are harmful for us, and may cause us to sin by not forgiving someone. (We'll talk more about Forgiveness later in F4.)

God also offers us another way to deal with our frustration and anger by taking it to Him:

> Complain if you must, but don't lash out. Keep your mouth shut, and let your heart do the talking. Build your case before God and wait for His verdict. Psalm 4:4

After we've taken our anger and complaints to God, wait for Him to respond, dear sisters. It's likely His response will come with a new peace about what happened—perhaps through a Scripture He brings to your mind, or through something you read in your Bible or a Christian devotional.

Once God has responded, dear sisters, you will know what to do with your feelings.

Let's end with what Joyce Meyer, well known Christian author and speaker, says about anger:

"Is all anger sin? No, but some of it is. Even God Himself has righteous anger against sin, injustice, rebellion and pettiness. Anger sometimes serves a useful purpose, so it isn't necessarily always a sin. Obviously, we're going to have adverse feelings, or God wouldn't have needed to provide the fruit of self-control. Just being tempted to do something is not sin. It's when you don't resist the temptation, but do it anyway, that it becomes sin. God sometimes allow us to feel anger anyway, so we will recognize when we're being mistreated. But even when we experience true injustices in our lives, we must not vent our anger in an improper way. We must guard against allowing anger to drag us into sin."

Joyce Meyer cites the Amplified Bible, Classic Edition (AMPC) for the verse we just used, Ephesians 4:26-27:

> When angry, do not sin; do not ever let your wrath (your exasperation, your fury or indignation) last until the sun goes down. Leave no (such) room or foothold for the devil (give no opportunity to him). Refuse to

give the devil any opportunity to get a foothold in your life through anger.

- Journal now about any other thoughts you have on anger.

ALONENESS, SADNESS, AND GRIEF

When I was diagnosed with breast cancer, I missed my parents all over again, especially my mom. I loved both of my parents very much, and spent a lot of time with them, especially with Mom after Dad passed away.

I do not have any sisters, and my only brother had died a couple of years after my parents, and only two years before my diagnosis. I felt like an orphan. I had no close family still living.

Because I was young, I'm not sure I knew anyone who'd had breast cancer. This diagnosis brought up old feelings of loss and abandonment with my birth family, and I felt very alone. It took time to grieve this out all over again, but it was a very necessary part of my process of healing.

Is there a loss you need to grieve, dear sisters? Loss includes the deaths of people you love, jobs, divorces, friendships, money, homes, etc.

- As you think about this, do you feel alone or sad right now, dear sister? Use your Journal to write about your feelings. Give yourself permission to grieve more deeply about anything that comes up for you.

I finally found peace with my aloneness when I came to know that I am never, ever alone. God is always with me, and He is always with you.

WISDOM FROM THE WORD

The Lord is close to the brokenhearted; He rescues those whose spirits are crushed. Psalm 34:18

O Lord, You have searched me and known me. You know when I sit down and when I get up; You understand my thought from far off. You search my path and my lying down and are aware of all my ways. For there is not a word on my tongue, but behold, O Lord, You know it fully. Psalm 139:1-4 (MEV)

SHAME

Dear sisters, I share this piece of my "woundedness" with you very gingerly. Remember the thirteenth tumor discovered during the mastectomy? Writing this book triggered a flash of understanding, an opening up if you will, about what made this tumor—the largest one—so well hidden inside my body and my soul.

> *I'd been carrying around an inner core of shame since I was a little girl, and didn't know it! I'd been burying it so far down inside myself, unconsciously trying to keep it from ever surfacing. Maybe I feared if it did—it would destroy me!*

It hurts my heart to type these words, but I'm already committed to being completely transparent with you. I will share anything I've uncovered, even what I've hidden from myself for so long, if it helps even one of you heal, dear sisters.

Here is what I wrote as I dissected that emotionally infected tumor lodged at the very core of who I thought I was:

> *Shame is a dirty feeling, a feeling that whatever is inside me is so innately flawed that I am rendered a filthy wrong mistake ... defective and unlovable. Unworthy of love.*

That is my core, and remnant shards are still with me today at age sixty-one. I have not been completely cleansed by Jesus because I have been unaware that total cleansing is my birthright as a Daughter of the Most High God—as we all are, my dear sisters—so I can be made whole by His never-failing love for me.

I have spent my entire life trying to cover up my shame-filled core of being unlovable by pleasing, performing, and silently pleading with others to love me because I was finally enough for them. This shame has been fueling my depression, oh Lord.

No wonder I thought God didn't, couldn't, wouldn't love me. I had been pronounced—in my own soul at least—unlovable. How could God possibly love me?

Digging deeper and deeper into the shame each morning, I sensed words only someone who loved me dearly—perhaps a loving parent or grandparent—would speak to me:

My dearest one, you have chosen to follow the only One who has made you worthy, our loving God. My daughter, oh my lovable daughter, He delights in you as the apple of His eye. He can never stop loving you, because His Son Jesus paid the price for your redemption over 2000 years ago, sweet child. Jesus paid it for you! Jesus endured both the pain and the shame of the cross for you, His precious daughter. His sacrifice for you made you perfect in God's sight because you accepted Jesus as your Savior. You finally quit trying to be your own savior by doing it all yourself, by performing and pleasing others as a way out of the shame you felt.

Dear daughter, Jesus would not allow Satan, the evil one, to shame Him. Because of this, Satan has no power to shame you, either, unless you believe his evil lies. I want you to know this: you are always free to choose to believe God's Truth instead.

I would tell you to scorn the shame and embrace His love, dear child. It is a healing balm for your soul, your body, *and your spirit. God loves you so, my sweet Suzanne. You have tried so hard to be loved, but His love for you is always there. It is your freely given birthright as His child.*

Will you accept this love that will never fail you? Will you also accept this truth as your birthright? You, my dearest one, can never be enough to fill anyone else's holes. Please lay down this horrible burden now. God would never, ever put that responsibility on you. Only God is enough, and He offers everyone His Holy Spirit to dwell in them, filling their holes completely, if they will only look to Him to do what only He can do: heal you completely in body, soul, and spirit.

Finally believing this, dear sisters, I screamed ferociously at the lie Satan, the "great deceiver," has told me all these years, the lie that has kept me from being close to emotionally healthy people; the lie that has kept me from choosing men committed to loving me for who I really am—not for what I could do or be in their lives; and the lie that has caused me to perform for love, perhaps missing what God had called me to do all along.

Oh, sweet sister, do you have your own tumor of shame inside you that doesn't belong to you? Are you willing to give that tumor of shame to Jesus right now? Are you ready to reject the shame, just as He did, because He does not see you worthy of shame? Do you believe instead you are worthy of the birthright of complete love He so freely gave to you from the cross?

If so, declare these Words of Wisdom from His Word out loud:

- I am forever free of condemnation. (Romans 8:1)
- I am assured that all things work together for my good. (Romans 8:28)
- I cannot be separated from the love of God. (Romans 8:35)
- I have not been given a spirit of fear, but of power, love, and self-discipline. (2 Timothy 1:7)
- I am born of God and the evil one cannot touch me. (1 John 5:4)
- I am God's temple. (I Corinthians 3:16)

- I am seated with Christ in the heavenly realm. (Ephesians 2:6)
- I can do all things through Christ who strengthens me! (Philippians 4:13)

Blessed be the name of the Lord for the many blessings He has given us! Amen!

A few days later, I wrote the following during my morning time with God. This is what I now believe and claim as my birthright. It is your birthright, too, dear sisters. Knowing and believing this allows us to heal more completely…

JESUS IS OUR SHAME COLLECTOR

I can be a very visual person, dear sisters, and often picture something I'm trying to deal with in prayer. When praying early one morning in bed, still half asleep, I had this beautiful dream-thought of the loving power of His love for us:

> In my mind's eye, I saw the long root of shame with all its infiltrating tentacles I'd just pulled out of my heart—leaving one large hole with many fissures and smaller roots trying to spread out everywhere.
>
> "How do I stop shame from spreading?" I cried out to the Lord in prayer. "The roots are pulled out, but the holes and furrows remain!"
>
> Continuing in my half-awake dream, I sensed Jesus holding out His right hand toward me, as if He was asking me to give Him the weed and its roots. Slowly handing it to Him—feeling like it weighed so much I might have to lay it down again—I was terrified when He saw it in its naked ugliness, He would totally reject me.
>
> Instead, I saw Him reaching out to me, holding a cup with His blood He'd shed for my sins and my healing. Somehow, I knew He wanted me to pour it into the holes.

Yet I stood there, hesitantly questioning Him with my eyes.

Suddenly I understood that His blood also symbolizes His love, freely given, for my complete healing. Only then could I give Him my hurts, my pain, and my failures. He took them from me, permanently removing them from both of us. Feeling freer, I poured His love into all my now-empty holes. It made me whole again, exactly as Jesus created me to be: a living soul in a physical body with an eternal spirit.

Oh, dear sisters, God's love is what heals us, but we must be willing to give up our hurts, our pains, and even our cancerous tumors to Him. We must also be willing to trust Jesus with our darkest secrets we've kept well hidden inside our most vulnerable places—the very holes of our hearts.

The eyes of my heart could clearly see that when we allow Jesus to knit us back together in the places where the arrows of life have wounded us, we are also allowing Him to show us our true selves—the way He sees us through His eyes: chosen, beloved, precious jewels created by Him to live in fellowship with Him above all else. Only through Jesus' loving eyes can we see the beauty of His workmanship in us, and know we can never be separated from His great love for us.

Oh, sweet sisters, Jesus is continually collecting the weeds of shame and discouragement planted by Satan in our vulnerable and weary hearts. If we will give these weeds to Jesus, He will send them to the fatal ground of hell, where they will flourish without harming us any longer.

Are you willing to pray this prayer with me now, giving Him your shame?

Dear Jesus: I freely, gratefully, and wholeheartedly give You my shame, which You have already scorned for me as my Savior. You have rejected the shame, and You have cleansed

me white as snow, oh Holy One, as only You can do! Yes,
I declare with You that You have taken away my shame,
my sins, my mistakes, and my shortcomings, oh Lord. You
present me to Your Father with Your own sacrifice covering
me, and I am healed! Amen and Amen! Blessed be Your
Name, my Holy King. Amen!

When we allow our shame to be removed by the blood of Jesus, sweet sisters, the flower garden of our hearts will burst forth in healthy blooms of love, joy, peace, patience, kindness, goodness, faithfulness, gentleness, and self-control. These are the gifts of His Holy Spirit that will replace Satan's poison of shame in our souls! Praise His Holy Name!

THE BLEEDING WOMAN AND SHAME

As mentioned under F1: Faith, the bleeding woman would have felt shamed because she would have been ostracized from her family and her "church." When a woman experienced menstrual bleeding during Old Testament times, she was considered spiritually unclean. Others would be made unclean by touching her or her garments.

And yet, go here with me again please, she was bold enough to reach out on her own behalf and touch Jesus! Not only was that taboo by society rules for any woman, it was especially frowned upon—to the point of death—for an unclean woman in Biblical times.

And yet she dared to reach out her fingertips amid a crushing crowd of people following Jesus, and touch the fringes of His robe.

Why would she risk her very life to touch Jesus?

Because she knew if she could just touch His robe, she would be healed. In her shame and rejection as a social outcast who was considered "unclean," she still knew who Jesus was. She knew He was God, the *Jehovah Rapha*, who could heal anyone who believed in Him. She knew He was her last hope for healing. She knew Jesus was the only one who could finally make her clean and whole in body, soul, and spirit.

It was enough to make her dare to reach out in faith.

How many times have you reached out in faith, sweet sisters, knowing that God was the only One who could possibly heal you, save you, and give you hope for the unknown walk ahead?

This was my first time. In my desperation, just like the bleeding woman, I saw Jesus as my only hope. When I reached out to Him, the desperate cry of my heart touched the Savior's own loving heart, and He healed me for all eternity.

Although I was alive, it was knowing that I was healed in the way that meant my spirit would never die that carried me through the rough road ahead. I began to learn where I would spend eternity; I began to learn of a loving God who would never leave me.

For someone who had been abandoned emotionally and physically in life, and treated like a dirty child who was untouchable, I was made completely clean in His sight. A lofty thought I know, but the only one that offered me real peace and healed me whole—body, soul, and spirit.

God wants to do the same for you, my dear sister.

WISDOM FROM THE WORD

Instead of your shame you will receive a double portion, and instead of disgrace you will rejoice in your inheritance. And so, you will inherit a double portion in your land, and everlasting joy will be yours. Isaiah 61:7 (NIV)

Looking to Jesus, the founder and perfecter of our faith, who for the joy that was set before Him endured the cross, despising the shame, and is seated at the right hand of the throne of God. Hebrews 12:2 (ESV)

For the Scripture says, "Everyone who believes in Him will not be put to shame." (ESV)

O Lord, let me not be put to shame, for I call upon you... Psalm 31:17 (ESV)

But You, O Lord, are a shield about me, my glory, and the lifter of my head. Psalm 3:3 (ESV)

THE AFTER-STORY: THE LOVE THAT HEALS

Dear sisters, you must know I only became completely ready to look at the tumor full of shame when I accepted—came to know actually—I was wholly loved by God. This is what I learned during this long—often steep—part of the walk:

Pure, unconditional love is the most basic need of our soul and our spirit. This is the only love that will heal us completely: body, soul, and spirit.

Sometimes we settle for whatever love we can get: counterfeit love, conditional love, attempts at love, even very dysfunctional love that hurts, but nothing can fill the most basic longing of our souls like real, unconditional love.

Nothing.

There is only one source of pure, unconditional love that will never fail us or leave us, and that is God.

It took me most of my life to understand this important truth: only the heart that believes God exists and that He is a loving God can feel this unconditional love.

God's love is the love that heals and sustains us. God's love is the love that sees us through the dark times of our life. God's love is the love that lasts forever.

God's love is real love, pure love, love you can always count on. This, dear sisters, is what this "God-love" is really like.

God speaks His love language to you in ways that are different for each of us. Gary Chapman, in his book, <u>God's Love Languages</u>, says this is how God makes sure we feel loved.

How would I, who felt so unlovable, so unworthy, so shameful know this?

God lets me feel the soft vibration of a cat's purr, a baby's milk face after nursing, the heart-kiss from a Bible verse I read that day, the sheer loveliness of a child lying heart to heart with me, a lovely unexpected flower growing in this high desert climate, a friend's word of encouragement, even a wet kiss of a sea lion on a concrete slab in Mexico. The soft pieces of everyday life, in the quiet moments of my time with Him when I sense His presence and know His love—this is how I know God's love.

After I was diagnosed, I desperately cried out to God that if He loved me, please give me a passage to hold onto, a message from His own Word that could give me a solid hope that I would live to raise our sons.

God gave me Mark 5:35. I've shared this part of my walk with you, but you don't yet know how that verse played out for me as I began my healing journey. God surrounded that verse with a peace that surpassed all human understanding at one of the darkest times of my life.

And He gave me hope again. Solid hope that lasted.

This, my dear sweet sister, is how much God really loves us. God will meet our immediate need for reassurance, but He will also leave the choice of whether to trust in Him, or not, up to us. We can choose to accept His love, or we can choose to look elsewhere.

God let me decide if I really wanted to get to know Him as He truly is, or if I wanted to continue looking for a "god" in every New Age thing that came along.

I chose to trust in Him. I got to know Him in a deeper way by searching for Him in all the right places this time, in places He put into my life now that I was willing to see them. I found Him in my Bible, in Bible Studies, at church, and through Christian friends He placed in my life. I found Him when I prayed. I found Him during walks in nature, and in a 12-Step Program filled with people actively pursuing a deeper understanding of God. The people in Al-Anon meetings showed me the true God, a God who loves each of us with a love that filled the empty holes in our hearts.

I came to understand that having free choice in a fallen world included a life that would have ups and downs. Becoming a follower of Jesus as my Lord and Savior didn't give me a perfect life, but what it did do was give me a place to live for all eternity whenever I die.

Let's pause now, and get out our Journals. Give some thought as to who you really think God is deep down in your heart. It's okay to be boldly honest here, dear sisters. God wants to heal any mistaken ideas you have about Him.

- Do you see God as a loving God?
- Do you see yourself as lovable?
- Do you believe God loves you, just as you are right now?

Take as much time as you need to answer these questions.

Sometimes when we have a hard time believing God loves us, it is because we are afraid of Him, or we see Him as a punishing God. It took me a long, long time to believe that I was lovable, and that God could truly love me. As I mentioned earlier, a class called "Soulwork" (see Resources) helped me take a much deeper look at what I believed about God. After I clarified my beliefs in writing, the facilitator helped me discover whether my beliefs were supported by Scripture or not.

I had so many false beliefs it was no wonder I'd left the faith of my childhood to search for a different, more loving God. What a gift to finally believe Truth instead of what the world and my mind had been telling me!

★★★

Sweet sister, there is only one way for you to have real hope in your life, and that is to know in your very soul that God loves you. You will truly begin to know this when you allow yourself to feel His love. This is what heals you wholly—body, soul, and spirit—as you walk out this cancer journey. Knowing just how much God truly loves us can make up for the lack of love, affection, validation, or support we get from our relationships with other people.

Now here's the hard part: most of us are too wounded or battered by a parent or spouse who was "supposed" to love us, that we cannot believe that God loves us just as we are. We do not have to do something to "earn" His love; He loves us simply because He created us, and we are His children.

Dear sisters, there is nothing we can do to earn or deserve His love. Nothing.

Wow! This makes my heart beat rapidly and nervously. How could anyone love me just because I am, without me *doing something* to earn it? This is when I must quiet my mind and allow my heart to feel God's love for me. *Knowing* God loves me is the head thing. *Feeling* God's love for me is what heals me.

Here's an exercise to help you fully allow yourself to feel His love for you. Read this statement aloud several times so it goes deep into your heart:

"God loves me just because I am me."

Now breathe that love in, hold it, and then breathe it out gently and slowly. Take another deep breath into your stomach area, and then gently pull that breath up through your rib cage and into your chest area where your wounded heart is, and let your heart feel its goodness. Then gently release it.

Repeat. Keep breathing God's love in, surrounding your heart with His love for 10 seconds before releasing your breath. Repeat this daily during your journey, knowing that God's love is as constant as your breath. God will always love you, no matter what you do. He rejects your sins, but He never rejects you.

Romans 8:38 tells us:

> And I am convinced that nothing can ever separate us from God's love. Neither death nor life, neither angels nor demons, neither our fears for today nor our worries about tomorrow—not even the powers of hell can separate us from God's love.

Dear sisters, I share with you two important pieces of my own healing that are also true for you, if you will take hold of them:

- This is the core belief that heals our spirit: we believe in a God who loves us just the way we are right now.
- When I allow myself to both trust and feel God's love for me, I'm able to confess my sins to Him, confident the sins are removed from me forever.

This part of my walk was a long uphill climb I had to take slowly, one small step at a time, as my trust in Him began to build, dear sisters. Keep in mind that the important thing is that you are willing to allow yourself to feel His love with every step.

★★★

When we've dug deep enough inside ourselves, dear sisters, isn't the cry of our hearts: "Love me just as I am? Don't make me earn your love, or be worthy of your love because I've pleased you, or because I've done enough for you. Please just love me as I am."

Only God can completely answer the deepest cry of our hearts. I know that sometimes it's hard to believe that God loves us—you and me. If we grew up with parents that didn't always make us feel secure or protected, or who didn't know how to show love or affection to us, we learn to think we are unlovable, that something is innately wrong with us. Maybe we date, marry, or become good friends with someone who isn't very loving because that's what feels comfortable for us. We can also feel betrayed by someone we trusted, or we can feel abandoned by someone who wasn't there physically or emotionally for us.

Any of these can make us think we are unlovable, unless someone else is pouring real love into our hearts. For me, it had to start with God. Maybe that is how I am wired. Maybe that is how you are wired, too, dear sister. Only God can fill the God-sized hole inside of our souls with His love.

> I finally got to the end of myself, after trying everything I could think of to earn love, and just gave up. I felt hopeless and unlovable, dear sisters. When I finally turned to God and admitted I needed His help, He was waiting for me with wide-open arms. He'd been there all along, patiently waiting for me all those years.
>
> And I wonder, what have I missed, oh Lord? Your open arms, Your face, Your heart, Your love, Your forgiveness. Oh, my Abba Father (Papa), I am very sorry it took me so long to really know You!

Choosing God is the first step to complete healing and freedom, sweet sisters. He is standing at the door of your heart, knocking gently so as not to intrude. Will you open the door, and invite Him in, or will you just turn up the noise of your mind so you can't hear His patient, steady knocking?

I regret shutting the door, even unconsciously, before my diagnosis, but I can confidently say that deciding to open the door to my heart to God is the best decision I've ever made. It made such an important difference in my life when I finally understood what Jesus wants each of us to know:

> "Look! I stand at the door and knock. If you hear My voice and open the door, I will come in, and we will share a meal together as friends." Revelations 3:20

★★★

We've covered a lot of feelings, my friends. Are others coming up for you now? Pause now and take out your Journal.

- Write about any other feelings that are coming up for you right now before moving on to the next F, Family. Take as much time as you need. This is important for your healing.

Let's close with a quote from Corrie Ten Boom, Holocaust Survivor, in the devotional 365 Day Brighteners on Worry:

> "Worry does not empty tomorrow of its sorrow; it empties today of its strength."

F3: FAMILY

So much of who we are comes from our upbringing. Our most impactful relationships, for better or for worse, usually revolve around family. Our family has helped shape our opinion of ourselves, of God, and of the world around us.

Let that last statement soak in for a few moments, please, and then answer these questions:

- How do you define family?
- How has your family shaped your opinion of yourself? Of God? Of the world?

Write your immediate responses to these questions in your Journal.

★★★

You may have mentioned friends in your own definition of family. Because my birth family had already passed away, I thought of several long-time friends from the Midwest as my "family." When Al and I met, his family lived on the other side of the country, so I didn't know them very well.

When I talk to other sisters, they often say: "My best friend from childhood is like a sister to me." "My aunt is like a mom to me." "My grandparents raised me." "My best friend's mom or dad is like a second parent to me." "I have a strong church family to support me."

- Do you have someone like this in your life? Give this some thought in your Journal now.

★★★

The word family is traditionally defined as the people you are related to by blood or adoption. We usually refer to them as relatives. If you marry, your family expands to include your spouse, his relatives, and any children you have. This is the primary definition the Bible uses, but the Bible also cites Jesus saying the people who walk with Him become His family, too:

> He pointed to His disciples. "Look!" He said, "these are my mother and brothers." Then He added, "Anyone who obeys my Father in heaven is My brother, sister, and mother." Matthew 12:49-50 (TLB)

Does knowing this change your opinion of who your family is? Pick up your Journal again. Keep in mind there are no right or wrong answers as you write out your responses:

- What thoughts first come to mind when you think about your family?
- Are they—or were they—able to be of support to you during your cancer journey?

Keep in mind that support can come in many ways: spending time with you; taking you to doctor appointments; providing meals, babysitting, phone calls, or texts; bringing you gifts of flowers and books; offering you prayer support and/or financial support; or purchasing plane tickets so you can visit them for a vacation when you are able, etc.

★★★

Dear sisters, when you are going through a difficult time such as cancer, family is usually the first place you look for support. Ideally this is the strongest unit of support for us.

But sometimes it isn't.

As we take a closer look at our families, we may find we must redefine "family" for us to be able to heal physically, mentally, and spiritually. This is normal; many sisters find they need to do this. If your family isn't available for some reason (death, age, distance, previous issues or conflicts, etc.), you will also need to expand your concept of family for your own well-being.

Expectations for our families and friends can also leave us disappointed if we expect something from them that they usually wouldn't do. For example, if your parents usually show support by doing things for you or sending money, rather than emotionally supporting you, they probably won't suddenly become the emotionally present parents you want them to be just because you have cancer.

However—and this is important for your healing—right now that is okay! We must, for our own sake, look elsewhere for any support our family is not able to give us. I know this isn't easy to do, dear sisters. It takes courage on our parts. You may think you can go through this alone, but please do not even try, dear sisters.

> When I had cancer, we had two young sons. My husband's role was to go to appointments with me as a second set of ears, and he also took excellent care of our young sons, allowing me the time and energy to heal. He even found the place I went for alternative treatment.
>
> He did not sit on the sofa with me and cry, or profess great love and understanding. I would have liked some of this, but it is not his way.
>
> And I came to understand that is okay.
>
> Others filled in the emotional gaps. Two best friends, Lilli Ann and Carol, went with me for different weeks during my alternative treatments. What a generous gift! We shared some laughter in what could have been a very depressing

situation for me, and Al kept the boys secure and happy at home, another much needed gift for me. I am forever grateful to my friends for taking time out of their busy work lives to be with me. Again, what a gift!

Then a dear friend, who is a R.N. finishing her PhD at the time, came to Flagstaff to bring me home from the hospital. Dr. Margie was the perfect person to care for me during those difficult first days following a mastectomy and tram-flap reconstruction. She even baked Sam and Andy homemade cookies and read to them. I will never forget her loving kindness that helped me heal.

Another friend, Nixie, left her young son with her parents, and came out to stay with me after Margie left. She took me to my follow-up appointments, and gave me such loving and fun support. She was a wonderful person to talk things over with, and she helped me look forward to more great times in our friendship when I felt better.

Al's family offered loving support through cards, books, letters, flowers, and calls. His parents sent plane tickets to come to Florida for Easter when treatment was over. This was another form of support that I appreciated. It gave me something fun to look forward to.

Al's brother, Bob, sent me a book by Lance Armstrong, <u>It's Not About the Bike: My Journey Back to Life</u>, right after I was diagnosed. I devoured this book of generic hope because Lance's cancer was far worse than mine, and he was alive and bike racing again. Encouraging stories of survivors are such blessings and another much needed form of support.

Let's pause now and return to our Journals.

- Write down any further thoughts you have about those who have been a support to you. If you don't look to family for support, give some thought to the reasons why you don't. Being very honest here will help your own healing, dear sisters.

We'll talk about how to heal this "dis-ease" or "un-ease" with our own families in the next section, F4: Forgiveness.

★★★

At the beginning of my cancer walk, I tried to go it alone. Fortunately, I soon realized the importance of talking with others with cancer or who had knowledge of treatment options, as I went to appointments and met other sisters. I learned that support groups are a good idea, but talking with one other survivor who has a good attitude also works well. If you can do both, I would encourage you to do so.

Husbands, family members, and even best friends are not always able to understand and offer you support like other survivors can. They can be too full of fear, or too close to you, or want you to soldier on so their lives are not affected by your disease.

I had to learn—sometimes the hard way—that this was okay, so I wouldn't expect support from those who didn't have it to give. I had to stop doing this for my own sake and for my own healing. Maybe you will avoid expecting too much from someone, too, for your own well-being, sweet sisters.

★★★

I have seen the benefit of reaching out and accepting friendship and help in so many sisters' lives, I encourage you once again to not go through this breast cancer walk alone. There are so many other areas of support you can rely on, such as:

1. **Your extended family**, the people you feel closest to, who aren't relatives.
2. **Neighbors**.
3. **Co-workers or members** of any groups you belong to.
4. **People (often other survivors) that suddenly show up in your life**. As the word gets out, friends may introduce you to other people who have had breast cancer. Because you share

a common bond, you may become friends for a season—or a lifetime. Either way is a plus!

5. **People you meet through your local Cancer Center.** There are usually cancer support groups run by the center, and they often include social workers or counselors. I met Doris, who was diagnosed around the same time I was, through a new wellness group we both joined. It was such a blessing to have a "buddy" through this process, and I also cherish the love and support shown to me by the group. Blessed women!

   Do you have someone you can **"buddy up"** with? This could include someone who is already done with treatment too. Be open to this possibility, and ask others if they know of someone if you don't. Reaching out is critical for your healing, dear sister.

6. **The program "Reach to Recovery"** is available in many areas through the American Cancer Society (ACS). Survivor sisters will come by to visit you in the hospital or meet you somewhere. They can answer your questions and offer you hope and support. Ask about this program in the hospital or office where you are being treated, or contact your local ACS.

7. If you are unable to attend a local support group, you can join an **online support group.** "Google" *online breast cancer support group,* or log onto "Facebook," and do the same search. Please use good judgment before joining any available groups. Not all sites are legitimately helpful.

8. **Your medical team.** The nurse coordinator for treatment at our local cancer center is a breast cancer survivor herself. She has offered guidance and support to the women who have met with her as part of their treatment. The staff where you choose to be treated may also know of local areas of support for you.

9. **Your church family,** if you are involved with a church. If you aren't involved in a church, now is a good time to get started. Cancer helped me return to a solid Christian church and faith. My closest friendships are now with the women I worship

with every week, and spend time with during Bible Studies or Neighborhood Group.

10. **Books** written by or about other survivors, such as this book.

- Feel free to add any additional areas you think of in your Journal now.

I have been on the walk for many years now, sweet sisters, and I believe God puts people in our path to help us. Do not be afraid to ask for help, or to accept help.

Before you launch into a sister's usual refrain: "I can't accept help. I can never repay someone …" Stop!

Yes, stop!

You, without choosing to, have joined a sisterhood made up of good, kind women. It can be this group you never signed up for that offers you the most hope and understanding. Accept all healthy offers of help. You, too, can show your thanks by "paying it forward" when you are well.

Right now, your only "service work" is to allow yourself the time and self-focus to get well.

- Let's take some time now to journal about ways you have connected. If you haven't reached out yet, note any of the previous suggestions you want to implement in your own healing walk.

QUESTION: WHO IN OUR FAMILY CAN WE ALWAYS RELY ON?

Answer: "Our Father in heaven …" Matthew 6:9 (NIV)

Dear sisters, what if we were taught these Truths from the Bible, and we grew up believing: *"God is my Father, He loves me unconditionally, and He will never, ever stop loving me?"*

What if our parents had been able to say to us: *"Mom and Dad love you very much, but we are not always going to do everything right. We are going to make mistakes and mess up sometimes. But God, your heavenly Father, always gets things right. As the creator of the world and of you, His love is the most important love you will ever have. He loves you all the time, every day, no matter what you do. God will always be there for you."*

My life would have been very different. Would yours?

I must admit, I didn't teach this to my children or ever say it this way, but there is still time to say it to them now—and to my future grandchildren.

While many of us have the awareness of God as our Heavenly Father, perhaps we haven't taken this truth into our own hearts yet, and made it a real, tangible relationship between a Father and His daughter. We must allow our "head knowledge" to become our "heart knowledge," dear sisters, for us to really feel His love.

When I began to see God as my Heavenly Father, I started to feel His love and healing more deeply. I began to trust in Him. Why?

By spending time with Him, I came to know God as a very involved, caring, and reliable Father. Prayer, quiet time in the Word, journaling, going to church, listening to uplifting sermons on my phone or computer, and attending Bible studies and retreats all helped me begin to see Him as He was, not as "life" had led me to think He was.

Consider spending more time with God, dear sisters, so you, too, can come to know Him as your own loving Father.

WISDOM FROM THE WORD

Many of you have told me that God has sent you support in all types of "packages." Dear sisters, please know that we are never truly alone. If we feel we are alone, we can reach out to our Heavenly Father because He has said:

> ...Never will I leave you; never will I forsake you.
> Hebrews 13:5b (NIV)

When you reach out and allow others to help you, please know how Jesus views what His children do for others:

> For I was hungry and you gave Me food, I was thirsty and you gave Me drink, I was a stranger and you welcomed Me, I was naked and you clothed Me, I was sick and you visited Me, I was in prison and you came to Me."

> Then the righteous will answer Him, saying, "Lord, when did we see You hungry and feed You, or thirsty and give You drink? And when did we see You a stranger and welcome You, or naked and clothe You? And when did we see You sick or in prison and visit You?"

> And the King will answer them, "Truly, I say to you, as you did it to one of the least of these my brothers, you did it to Me." Matthew 25:35-40 (ESV)

Finally, for peace of mind regardless of what your family support is like, keep in mind our true family:

> See what kind of love the Father has given to us, that we should be called children of God; and so we are. 1 John 3:1a (ESV)

> And stretching out His hand toward His disciples, He said, "Here are My mother and My brothers! For whoever does the will of My Father in Heaven is My brother and sister and mother." Matthew 12:49-50 (ESV)

★★★

Before reading F4: Forgiveness, I suggest you spend some additional time journaling about your parents and the people you consider family. Two things usually happen when you do this, and I believe both are ultimately healing. You begin to realize the loving support that surrounds you now, and you begin to get in touch in a deeper way about issues you have in your own family.

Dearest sisters, I would tell you that until you are honest with yourself about issues with your family, you cannot begin to fully heal. My personal walk heavily involved the next F: Forgiveness, in ways that were hard for me to see in the beginning. Even though my birth family was dead, I was still carrying around buried resentments and bitterness about some of the things that happened—or didn't happen—in our family.

I think because I wouldn't deal with the issues in my own heart and forgive, the bitterness and resentments announced themselves through the buried cancerous tumors. An unusual thought, I know, but perhaps you have a sense of the same thing, dear sisters.

Since my birth family was no longer living, there was no way to resolve any of these issues by talking with them. Fortunately, there was a very important step I could still take, with God's help. It is called *forgiveness*.

This may be part of your own healing work, sweet sisters, in your personal journey to wellness. In our next chapter, F4: Forgiveness, we will be working on any difficult areas you have with your family or friends, however you defined F3: Family.

─── F4: FORGIVENESS ───

When I began to mentally dissect those tumors, I discovered that I had buried years of resentment and bitterness under so many hard, nearly impenetrable shells. I didn't even know they were there until my cancer diagnosis!

> *Left to my old ways of coping, I would have forcefully pushed this mess back down inside myself again, and put an even harder shell over it! I think there was something very comforting about holding onto my resentments!*
>
> *But I'd learned that God's way was very different than my human way of wanting to hang onto what I thought was the reason for my problems: that old refrain "somebody done me wrong."*
>
> *I had my mental list of my "somebodies" and their wrongs, and I knew it well. I even took family member's deaths personally, as in "They abandoned me! I'm so hurt!" Each "wrong" or "hurt" had its own tumor, I was certain. I could tell that not forgiving the "somebodies" was making me sick!*

And yet I found forgiveness was so hard for me to do on my own, dear sisters. When I chose to look at what God says about forgiveness, I was finally able to do the hard work of forgiving.

WISDOM FROM THE WORD

There are many verses about forgiveness in the Bible, but there were two that clearly had a very direct impact on me. The first is taken from the Lord's Prayer. It might be familiar to you:

> "… and forgive us our sins, as we **have forgiven** those who sin against us." Matthew 6:12

Jesus further emphasizes this passage in verses 14 and 15:

> "If you forgive those who sin again you, your heavenly Father will forgive you. But if you refuse to forgive others, your Father will not forgive your sins."

I grimace as I write this, dear sisters. There is no quibbling about what Jesus meant. His words are direct and clear. I cannot be forgiven by God unless I forgive others. Jesus' use of the past tense, *have forgiven*, strongly suggests that we are expected to forgive others first.

Then God forgives us.

Jesus offers a message further clarifying the importance of forgiving others in Matthew 18:21-22:

> Then Peter came to Him and asked, "Lord, how often should I forgive someone who sins against me? Seven times?"

> "No, not seven times," Jesus replied, "but seventy times seven!"

With these two Scriptures speaking so clearly about the importance Jesus places on us forgiving others, just as He forgives us, I knew I needed to pay attention to this "F" in an important way for my own healing.

In other words, I needed to do it God's way, not my way!

WHAT IS FORGIVENESS?

What is forgiveness, sweet sisters? The dictionary defines it as "the act of pardoning somebody for a mistake or wrongdoing." "Mercy" is one of the words listed as a synonym for forgiveness. Since mercy means giving someone undeserved favor, this tells us that we should forgive even when we think the other person doesn't deserve it.

This agrees with what God has just revealed to us in Scripture, doesn't it?

"Blame" is cited as the antonym (opposite) of forgiveness. Blame is exactly what I most want to do when I won't forgive someone. I want to blame him or her for what happened, and not look at my part in it. And I sure don't want to take responsibility for what I did, or might be doing.

I did this for too many years with my ex-husband. I wanted to blame him for our marriage falling apart. Yes, there are things he'd done that were wrong, but there were things I'd done that were wrong, too. We were both at fault.

To look at my part in a failed marriage required honesty and a certain amount of maturity from me. I didn't want to go there for years. By having someone to blame, I could feel entitled to hang onto my feeble self-esteem, despite feeling very rejected and unlovable. I felt abandoned or "punished" for not doing what he demanded I do that was morally wrong for me. Our marriage ended soon after that.

Oh, dear sisters, I could go on and on about this, but the truth of the matter is I have forgiven him, and I hope he has forgiven me. It's been over twenty-seven years since the divorce; I've remarried, and we have two adult children now. My ex-husband has remarried, too. I think it's time I prayed for God's best for them, and let it go. And I have.

Praying for God's best for someone I don't want to fully forgive is a step I've found that makes a big difference for me when I want to go back to "not forgiving" again. Instead of letting Satan get a toe-hold in my head and heart by replaying any old tapes or the "somebody done me wrong" refrain yet again, I can choose to pray for God's best for that person and let it go.

This, too, leads to the place of "peace which exceeds anything we can understand" (Philippians 4:7b) that is so necessary for my spiritual and mental health.

Yours, too, sweet sister.

Looking back, I see that for much of my adult life after my mother died, I spent a lot of time still hoping to get what I wished I could have received from her. I wanted outward signs of being loved by her in my childhood, so I didn't feel like a bother or too needy. Because of the alcoholism in our family with Grandpa and then my brother, combined with our entire family's attempts at burying it inside or sweeping it under the proverbial rug, I didn't get this.

During my prayer walk this morning, an odd memory came back to me. I was asking God for help with clarity and to know His will regarding this part of forgiveness, and I suddenly remembered something my mom said when she was mad or upset with someone (although she never admitted she was mad).

It went something like this: "When I'm done with someone, I'm done." Nothing was ever explained, but I thought I could see she "was done with" a relative. I liked this relative very much, so I couldn't see why Mom and her sister had little to do with this other relative. Since we never talked about anything, I couldn't find a way to really ask her why at my young age. This left me fearful she would be done with me one day, with no warning and no explanation, and certainly no opportunity to work it out. This was very frightening to me as a young child.

To make sure that never happened, I began to try to earn her love. My pleasing behavior began. I found that if I excelled at school and didn't get into trouble, she was happy with me. I think this was influential in how I subconsciously chose to live my adult life.

When our families aren't there for us as children—usually due to death, addictions, work, or divorce—there is a huge void in our lives, dear sisters. We become "little adults" to try to take care of our own needs and sometimes theirs, too. I can personally say this behavior doesn't stop when we are adults, unfortunately, but it can get better.

It can be healed.

How can terrible situations get healed? By grieving for what we didn't have, dear sisters. By allowing ourselves to grieve honestly and fully for what we didn't have emotionally, or whatever happened to us, we will finally be able to move into a place of acceptance and forgiveness.

If a lot of emotions and memories are coming up for you, I'd encourage you to take a break from your reading now. Please don't avoid them. Instead take some time to rest and do something you enjoy, before you try to explore any areas where you still "hurt." It helps to write these out in your Journal, too.

If you'd like to express them aloud in a helpful way, please commit to spending some time with a therapist or in a 12-Step group, if that applies to you. Or talk it out with a trusted friend who can simply be a listening board. Choose the friend carefully, though, sweet sister, by making sure it's someone who is understanding and kind. Not every friend will be able to hear what we have to say, and that's okay. That's what counselors and support groups are for.

★★★

I could not fully heal until I began to forgive, dear sisters. And I couldn't forgive until I came to understand what forgiveness is and what it is not.

I had to be willing to "let go and let God" deal with the hurts, many of which I finally realized were not intentionally done to me. I had to become willing to walk out forgiveness as a gift to myself, something I did for my own healing, and because God asks me to be obedient to His Word.

Research strongly supports what God always knew is best for us. Harbored resentments and deeply buried anger at others breeds bitterness deep inside our very souls.

And that bitterness and hurt, dear sweet sisters, is what fuels tumors. At least, it was a significant part of mine.

I learned that when we choose to forgive someone, we are not choosing to trust them again. Forgiving is something **we** choose to do. Earning our trust back is a choice **the other person** makes. He or she might not even try to earn our trust again, so we shouldn't have that expectation.

It takes a lot of energy to carry around anger, blame, and hate. It drains our own spirit, our own life force. It rips apart our soul, leaving us in emotional dis-ease.

We only have so much energy, dear sisters; it is not limitless. If we keep choosing to use our energy to ruminate on what someone else did to us, we won't have enough energy left to heal. We need to focus on our own healing, not on revenge, continued anger, or buried resentments at someone else.

My prayer is that you will be able to forgive so you can begin to heal, my dearest sweet sisters.

THE WALK OF FORGIVENESS

After repeatedly trying to forgive what I thought of as "mean actions against me," I finally came to the end of myself. I wore myself out rehashing the same old stuff, without being able to let go of it and move on. Now I can see how this was blocking my healing when I simply couldn't—or wasn't willing to—let go of certain things.

I came to understand that the buried resentments, which I could name and hold up like badges of wounding, kept feeding the tumor-producing seeds of bitterness. I felt justified in holding onto them, but it was me—not the other people—the resentments were hurting.

I thought what was important for my healing was to look again at the buried hurts of what I thought "had been done to me." Anything was fair game for me to take personally, and I tended to make everything someone did "about me." Embarrassing to admit, but true.

Yes, some deeply painful things were "done to me." Some things that felt painful probably weren't "done to me" at all. They were just done with no harm intended. Some personalities are "harsher" than I would like, and some people take out their own unhappiness on others while trying to make themselves feel or look better.

I know this because I have done some of it myself, especially with comparisons or judgments of others in my own head. Again, embarrassing to admit, but it is true.

By continuing to walk out my healing, I came to understand that much of what happened in my family of origin had no harmful or mean intent behind it. My parents were a product of the times they lived in; people worked hard and often didn't express softer emotions.

I was raised without very many hugs and kisses, or being told "I love you."

In fact, I don't remember getting any physical or emotional signs of affection. As a small child, I needed these physical and verbal expressions of love. I still do as an adult. Around my mid-twenties, I decided to start giving my mom a kiss on the cheek. Hopefully I also said, "I love you" to her whenever I said goodbye. With no return hug or kiss from her, although she willingly offered me her cheek to kiss, I finally asked her one day why she didn't ever return the hug or kiss.

Her reply probably spoke volumes: "Because my mother told me if you ever hug or kiss someone you love goodbye, you will never see them again."

I wish I would have had the courage to ask where that silly belief came from. Now it's too late to ask. I can only guess that someone in a previous generation must have died after a hug or kiss goodbye—perhaps in war or something equally tragic—and that "advice" got passed down through the generations.

My mom suffered many miscarriages before she had me. She also gave birth to a stillborn son, my brother Timothy, a year before she had me. When she went into labor with me, the doctor came out to the waiting room and told my dad he would lose either my mom or me during birthing, because I wouldn't "come out."

I think the doctor even asked my dad to choose which one of us he wanted him to save!

I cannot imagine being asked such a question! That's so far from a happy birthing experience for my parents! I never heard how—or if—my dad could answer such a question, but eventually I was pulled out by forceps, and we both lived.

Would any of my mother's birth experiences have caused her to be afraid she'd lose me, so she protected her soft heart? I will never know, but I would guess this affected all of us.

I have finally come to see that while healthy families show many signs of love to their children, my family just didn't know how to do this. They probably craved the same things I did: hugs and closeness, and words of love expressed aloud, but they didn't get these from their parents either.

What's important today is I can finally believe they loved me, and I can recognize how they showed their love for me in non-demonstrative ways. By choosing to forgive, I can feel their love again, and see them for the good people they both truly were.

Sometimes I wonder if I didn't forgive them for so long, so I wouldn't miss them as much. Maybe I was more comfortable "resenting them" than "missing them." Unhealthy as this sounds, being angry feels more powerful than the raw painfulness of missing them, because I know there is nothing I can do to bring them back.

One of the saddest things in my life has been for my children not to know my parents. Dad would have delighted in my two sons, and patiently showed them everything about the farm and the animals. They would have had a taste of what was great in my childhood—the outdoors, the animals, the tractor rides—the many good things about farm life.

Every 4th of July we would have shot off some small fireworks, eaten ice cold watermelon and spit out the seeds, and played with water guns in the front yard. A variety of pets would have been with us, unless we sprayed them with water!

I like to think Mom would have been more affectionate with her grandchildren. They would have brought that out in her, and it would have been healing for all of us.

And I'd like to imagine that they would have given my parents joy in what was a hard life, with not much of what I'd call pleasure or fun. The kids would have allowed them to have fresh hope that things would be better for these two boys, and they would have known the love and funny moments Sam and Andy would have brought them.

In my heart, I can hear the peals of their laughter as they chased the dogs and cats and chickens around the green grass of the farm, and learned how to collect eggs with dad without getting pecked, and how to climb on the fence to look over at the cows. A delightful life I so wish had been part of their childhood! It nearly breaks my heart, even today, when I think of what my sons missed by not having grandparents who lived on a farm in rural Missouri.

I also think I could have had a different view of my childhood after watching my parents with the boys. I grieve for myself, and for Alan too. My parents would have really liked him. Al showered our sons with love and affection, kisses and hugs. I am so grateful to Al for showing me the way to relax with the boys and let my love for them be warmly expressed instead of held back in fear something would happen to them.

My parents were good people. They worked hard, they were kind, they helped others, and they were generous. They were humble and quiet, the salt of the earth. This is the memory I choose for myself today, and the memory I will carry with me on my walk. I am glad I was finally able to

grieve for what I missed; and for what Al, Sam, and Andy
missed by not having my parents in their lives.
Thank you, Jesus, for this healing!

Sweet sisters, that is a lot. My eyes are teary at finally being able, with God's help, to get to this place. How about you? Did reading this trigger any memories for you, or bring up areas that need forgiveness, or remind you of the people you've already forgiven?

I know that some memories can't be made better by remembering what was good. Some hurts, like any type of abuse—physical, sexual, or verbal—will have no gifts to be remembered in them. Abuse is wrong on every level. These are deep wounds, and therapy is needed to help you heal. Please write about any types of abuse that apply to you, and please get help to deal with any deep wounds remaining in you.

I've been verbally abused by a person I love for my faith, the small college I attended, my intelligence (because I believe the Bible literally), and the part of the country where I grew up. I know firsthand someone's words can be very damaging, even when they are not based in truth. Every form of abuse is horrendously damaging to our very souls and spirits.

Dear sister, if you have been abused in any way, please seek professional help for your own sake. Wounds this deep can make it hard to know a loving God who offers you His healing love, or for you to have healthy relationships with others. It also makes it very hard to take good care of yourself, because you have been wrongly devalued by people you care about.

Please know that this type of abuse is not your fault, sweet sister, and you deserve to be able to allow yourself to heal from it. Please.

Pause now and begin writing about what comes up for you when you read this. Maybe it's a little, or maybe it's a lot, but always know anything is okay. It really is.

WHO DO I NEED TO FORGIVE?

When we sit down to write in our Journals about who we need to forgive, it can be less overwhelming and more clarifying to look at four separate areas where forgiveness could be needed:

- Forgiving Others
- Forgiving Yourself
- Forgiving God
- Asking God to Forgive You

Let's look at each one separately, and take the time to do whatever forgiveness work we need to do in each area with God's help.

FORGIVING OTHERS

Forgiving another person is an act of obedience to God's command for all of us. It does not make what the other person did right, nor does it make our feelings wrong. It simply means we chose to forgive because God tells us to forgive—whether we are right, or they are, or neither of us is!

Let's take another look at what Jesus told His disciples:

> "I tell you, you must forgive him more than seven times. You must forgive him even if he wrongs you seventy times seven." Matthew 18:22 (NCV)

Why would Jesus tell us to do something that is so hard for many of us? Because He knew that when we forgive, we set ourselves free. We allow our wounds to heal. We allow ourselves to feel God's inner peace, by keeping our focus on how we choose to live our lives instead of what someone else is doing or did. We are choosing life-giving freedom from the unhealthy emotions of blame and bitterness.

We must know that once we have forgiven someone, we will choose to let the past hurts or wrongs go whenever we remember them in the future. We must also remember that Jesus is there to help us choose to forgive "seventy times seven." It's one of the many gifts of having His Holy Spirit in us. On our own, forgiving is often very difficult because the hurt is very real.

We watched a video clip at church recently. It was about a woman who had recently lost her husband to a random killing. He was a new father, and a man of strong faith. It is a tragic story.

What was most remarkable about the story was the wife's faith. Her faith in God gave her such a peace the very same day this happened, and allowed her to instantly forgive the men who did it. The newscaster kept questioning how she could forgive so soon, finally asking her to help him understand.

She could only explain: "I don't understand. I just know I felt such a peace the day it happened. It was God's Spirit working in me. I wanted God's love to shine through me. I wanted the men who killed my husband to know that God loves them, too."

This woman was spot on in her understanding of God's level of forgiveness. She knew His Word, and most importantly, she knew God. She understood the words Jesus spoke to Peter about the necessity of forgiving, even when the forgiving cannot be understood in human terms.

I think she also knew something else God tells us about forgiveness in His Word that often gets overlooked: God tells us He forgives us for His own sake!

"I—yes, I alone—will blot out your sins for My own sake and will never think of them again." Isaiah 43:25

Could it be that God doesn't find it healthy or a good idea to carry around the remembrance of our sins against Him? Suddenly I see forgiving others in a new light: I have held onto so much negative energy by not forgiving those "done me wrongs," only hurting myself in the long run.

His Words are full of wisdom for living a healthy life in all ways: spiritually, emotionally, and physically. I, too, must forgive others for my own health and well-being.

> Consider the widow again. We can only imagine what her life would be like if she didn't choose to forgive those men who killed her husband in a random act of violence. Her child would have been robbed of two parents: one to death, and one to a living death of her very soul and spirit. The evil tragedy would have lived on even more painfully in their lives.

Sweet sisters, please know that when someone has truly done something wrong, forgiving them doesn't mean it is safe for you to be around them, or that what they did was right. It just means that you will finally be able to heal by forgiving them and moving on past the anger and resentment you are carrying around.

Always remember these Words from Jesus, sweet sisters:

> "The thief comes only to steal and kill and destroy; I have come that they may have life, and have it to the full." John 10:10 (NIV)

Forgiveness is one of the ways we can have this abundant and full life.

Pause now and give yourself some quiet time to reflect on who you might need to forgive. Knowing now that God wants us to forgive for our own sake, and that He forgives us when we forgive others, does that make a difference in your willingness to forgive?

> And be ye kind one to another, tenderhearted, forgiving one another, even as God for Christ's sake hath forgiven you. Ephesians 4:32 (KJ21)

Here are the steps to forgiveness, dear sisters:

- Writing it down in your Journal helps get it out, once and for all. Ask yourself: who are you still angry with? If the mention of someone's name causes you to tense up, spout off, or respond negatively (outwardly or inwardly), it is giving you a strong signal you are holding on to negative feelings about him or her. Who is that person?

- Release the offense. Let it go. "Leave it" is a command I give to our dog when I want her to let go of something, turn away from it, and move on. It's a simple command that calls for obedience right then. It works! When I find myself thinking negative or mean and angry thoughts about someone now, I hear these words in my own mind: "Leave it." It causes me to pause, take a quick inventory on what I'm feeling, and release it to God. Spend some time now journaling about what you might need to leave behind or release.

- Forgive the person or persons. Remember you are doing it for your own sake. Pent up anger, resentment, and bitterness from not forgiving aren't good for us. If we truly want to heal, we need to release what happened to God to handle. God tells us in Romans 12:19b: "Vengeance is Mine." His, not ours, dear sisters! If whatever someone else did to you was a sin, then that is between that person and God.

We are not to judge; that is God's job. The simple 12-Step slogan "Let go and let God" helps me surrender those feelings to Him.

As I've walked out my faith and my healing over seventeen years, I've learned to see others in a softer light; they too are often broken and hurting. To be able to do this, however, I had to acknowledge my own brokenness and hurts, and come to realize that it is okay for me to feel this way. It's also okay to share them with a person who understands and does not judge. Breast cancer support groups may offer this; a 12-step group can also be a safe place. So is journaling and talking it out with God through your writing, and by reading His Word. A good therapist can be a wonderful help, too. Your church may offer this service or be able to refer you to someone who is qualified to help you.

When I refuse to forgive someone (whether they apologize for their "offense to me" or not), I am allowing a seed of bitterness (a long-held resentment) to take hold inside me. My buried anger or hate over what they "did" to me may never be resolved with them in person. They may be dead, unreachable, or refuse to talk to me.

What's important for my own healing and well-being is that I make the choice to forgive them, and give what happened to God. Allowing God's armor of protection to surround me with His love helps shield me from further hurts.

It is a fact of life, dear sisters, that people will hurt us, often unintentionally, and sometimes intentionally. It may simply be they "want whatever they want," and that may involve leaving us, hurting us, shaming us, or other painful actions. This is not right, but it happens.

Keep in mind this truth, dear sisters: we are all hurting people, including the person who hurt you. In our own pain, we sometimes hurt others in a misguided attempt to make ourselves feel better. We also hurt others out of anger, hate, resentment, selfishness—the list is extensive. Again, this isn't right, but it happens.

There is wisdom in a statement from my graduate school counseling classes: "Hurt people hurt people."

For us to heal, sweet sisters, we must release this buried anger. If we don't, it can turn into cancerous tumors in our breasts—the feminine parts of our bodies that nurture babies, and cover our hearts. It can kill us—or wound us terribly emotionally, spiritually, and finally physically–if we don't forgive and let it go.

Do this forgiveness work for your own benefit because you are so worth it! You are a daughter of the "most high" God. He wants you to know who you are. I want you to know it too. It makes such a difference in your healing.

FORGIVING OURSELVES

The next step in the forgiveness process is forgiving ourselves. After we forgive someone else, we sometimes discover we are also angry at ourselves. Because God remembers my sins no more, I should also forgive myself.

I didn't even consider the possibility of forgiving myself until I joined a 12-step program after my alcoholic brother died at age thirty-eight. As I worked the 12-steps with my sponsor as part of my healing from the effects of growing up with active alcoholism in the home, I came to Step Eight. This step is called "the making amends step." At this point, we are encouraged to make a list of all the people we have harmed, and to apologize for our own actions whenever we can do so without causing them any more harm.

We are reminded to include ourselves on the list. We blame ourselves, sometimes for things that are not our fault, and it is vitally important that we extend the same forgiveness in love to ourselves that we are learning to extend to others. We need to learn how to treat ourselves with the same loving kindness that Jesus shows to us.

Part of my continued amends to myself is to actively choose more positive people to spend time with. Instead of hanging onto people who don't really seem to like me because I am afraid of being alone or without "family," I need to let them go in love and move on. This sets me free to seek out new, more loving friendships. I think it's a reflection of my own healing. It can be for yours as well, sweet sister.

- Let's pause and spend some time writing in your Journal about any of the places where you need to forgive yourself. Consider what amends you can make to yourself.

FORGIVING GOD

Sometimes we blame God for what goes wrong in our lives. We ask, "Why me, God?" when what we really want to know is: "Why are You doing this to me anyway, God?" I confess I sometimes thought of God as an angry God, just sitting up in Heaven with a zapper gun ready to zap anything I did that displeased Him.

I would guess a psychiatrist, or an unbeliever, could have a heyday with that one! By believing this lie about God, I was left with the false belief that God didn't love me. I thought I'd made too many "mistakes" for anyone to love me. I learned that people just abandoned me when I "needed" them, or tried to get close to them. Why wouldn't God abandon me, too? This is what I'd learned to believe from my life.

I cringe now at how unhealthy that sounds. Oh, sweet sister, I am baring my soul again in the hopes it will release or uncork emotions you've buried or hidden away so you, too, can heal. The deeply embedded thought that God was punishing me wouldn't leave until I learned Truth. My hope is that you, too, will embrace this Truth for yourself!

WISDOM FROM THE WORD

Here is the Truth I learned:

- "God is love." God loves us because He is love. (1 John 4:8b; John 3:16a)
- I am His child. (1 John 3:1)
- He created me by knitting me together in my mother's womb. (Psalm 139:13)
- He wants a deeply personal relationship with me. (Revelation 3:20)

I came to realize there is nothing to forgive God for. I didn't realize this until I was worn out from carrying around so much unexpressed blame and bitterness for so long, including my lengthy list of ways God, too, had let me down.

Sweet sisters, pause for a moment now, and write about ways you could be carrying around anger against God.

- Begin by asking yourself what you are angry with God about. Don't hide it deep inside you. Write it out in your Journal and take a good look at it.

Beat the bed with a cane if you need to. I've found by physically releasing my anger in an appropriate way, I can get down to the kernel of emotion buried underneath the anger.

What might be buried underneath your anger? Sometimes anger covers up fear, or shame, or self-blame. Sometimes it is simply anger. Ask God, and a counselor or support group, to help you work out your feelings.

Remind yourself it's okay to be angry, dear sisters. It really is. What gives us "dis-ease" is what we keep buried inside ourselves. Unresolved, suppressed anger at God can eat away at our souls each day. A dear friend, Pastor Peter, told me that God is strong enough to handle every bit of my anger.

Pastor Peter also told me if I would bring all my feelings to God, He could change my anger into a longing for more of Him. Peter promised that God wouldn't zap me or leave me.

Pastor Peter was right, dear sisters. God did not zap me or leave me. Instead, He opened His arms to me in love, allowing me to cry out my pain and frustration to Him. When I finished, He graciously replaced it with a peaceful understanding of His true, loving nature.

ASKING GOD FOR FORGIVENESS

Asking God for forgiveness is very healing. It is the step that finally sets us free to live the abundant life Jesus has for us—the abundant life that has no end when Heaven is our destiny!

As you ease into this, sweet sisters, ask yourself if there is anything that you have buried inside you that you would like to ask God to forgive.

After breast cancer, the boys and I started attending a Christian church in town. Friends had invited our boys to go to summer church camp with them, and I thought it would be a good idea for us to attend services at their church before they went.

After going to the church for a while, my heart began to feel like I was home: home with a God who had given me His Word to stand on when I was diagnosed, and home with the Christian faith my Grandmother shared with me when I was little. I was far from totally healed, but this felt like a good place to begin to deal with my spiritual wounding.

After several years of being part of this church, I began to feel a need to be baptized again. I'd already been baptized at the Christian church of my childhood, but it was a decision my parents made for me as an infant. There is absolutely nothing wrong with this way of baptism, but I felt a strong pull from within to make a new decision for myself, a commitment and a cleansing if you will. It felt like an important part of my repenting and accepting God's forgiveness for my past decision to walk away from Him.

After scheduling the baptism at church, buried memories started surfacing during my morning walks on the trails. I began to reflect on things I had done in the past when I wasn't walking with the Lord, and they brought up sadness, regret, and other strong emotions inside me. Sometimes I would go to the ground in tears and deep regret over choices I'd made that I knew were morally wrong.

I recognized this was my personal way of repenting. As I type this today, I remember the Scripture where the Lord says He doesn't want our fasting and our sacrifices, He wants our broken and repentant hearts:

The sacrifice you desire is a broken spirit. You will not reject a broken and repentant heart, O God. Psalm 51:17

God wants us to abandon the sin that separates us from Him. When we understand that something we've been doing or have done is sin, our spirits will feel broken. And the only way to heal our broken spirit is to repent of the sin to God, and walk away from repeating it in our lives.

Oh, dear sisters, I am not saying that I no longer sin. I am just saying that the sinful behavior that caused me to walk away from my Christian faith—all the mistakes that I'd made—have been confessed to God out of my broken, contrite (very sorry) heart, and I am committed to not repeating those mistakes. And I now know if I do repeat any of these mistakes, I should take them to God in repentance and remorse.

God's forgiveness—forgetting my sins completely—is what healed my broken soul and my broken spirit. I know He will heal yours, too, sweet sister, if you will come to Him in repentance.

★★★

How then do we ask God for forgiveness?

Begin by knowing this is not a hopeless process, sweet sisters.

It is never too late to ask God for forgiveness while we are still living, but there is everything to be gained by doing it now. His Word gives us a three-step approach for receiving His forgiveness that is straightforward and solid, but not easy:

- The first step involves admitting our wrongs by confessing them to God.
- The second step requires that we are truly sorry for our sins.
- The third step is equally essential to our healing: we must believe we are forgiven, trusting in God's promise to forgive us.

Once I got through the process of remembering and being sorry for my sins, God forgave me. This is not wishful thinking; God promises us His forgiveness in His Word. He lets our sins go—completely forgets them actually—when we confess them to Him and repent. Then it is our responsibility to trust in God's promise to us that He will forgive us (remove) our sins as far away as the "east is from the west."

> You see, God takes all our crimes—our seemingly inexhaustible sins—and removes them. As far as east is from the west, He removes them from us. Psalm 103:12 (VOICE)

How sweet it is to know we are forgiven, dear sisters! Will you accept this wonderful gift from your loving Father? Will you choose to believe the solid Truth of His Word that your sins have been removed from you as far as the east is from the west?

You are doing "big work" when you do take these steps, my friend. Let's pause now and reflect on this in our Journals.

- How are you feeling after repenting of any past sins? Write out your feelings or anything you want to get out of you now.
- Thank God for His complete forgiveness that sets you free.

★★★

As we end this section, know that we will probably never reach a level of not having to forgive someone for something again in our lifetime. It seems to be part of human nature in this fallen world.

As I continue to walk out forgiveness in my own life, I sometimes find I may forgive someone today, but tomorrow I may try to pick up the buried anger and resentments again.

I believe this is the work of Satan. He tries to cause us to lose our peace in Christ, to hold onto feelings that cause us to remove ourselves from God's presence, and to generally frustrate and annoy us in any way he can. We must do our part again, dear sisters, and stand firm against his efforts to drag us back into a place of unforgiveness.

Jesus Himself told Satan: "Get thee behind Me, Satan!" Matthew 16:23a (KJ21)

I often use those same words to put Satan back in his already defeated position. You, too, can use Jesus' powerful words to overcome Satan's tricks aimed at sending you right back into the sin of not forgiving. Remember God's Truth in Isaiah 55:11 (KJV): "My Word... shall not return to Me void." His Word always produces the results He intended.

***

The angels rejoice when we come to the Father, just as the father rejoiced when the prodigal son returned home. In Luke 15:11-32, Jesus tells His disciples about a wealthy father who had two sons. The eldest son faithfully worked for the father, but the younger son wanted his share of his inheritance immediately, so he could leave his family and do whatever he wanted to do. When the money ran out, he was homeless and hungry. Thinking about how even the workers at home got to eat something, he returned home. When the father saw him in the distance, he began planning a huge celebration because his lost son was home again.

The boys and I were baptized after church one day. It was an important personal decision for each of us. It was especially important to me to make this renewed commitment in the same way that Jesus did, by immersion, and it became a very healing part of my walk.

Perhaps even the angels rejoiced at my homecoming!

***

The third area of our healing, "Healing Your Body," is a very important part of walking out your wholeness, dear sisters. Although medical staff may focus on removing the cancer and using radiation and/or chemotherapy as their solution for healing the body, I've found that our physical healing takes place one day at a time, one step at a time, just like the other parts of our healing. It's a step I've personally continued to put emphasis on to prevent the physical cancer from coming back.

The first "F" in this section, Food, is one that had little emotional baggage for me. I'd already dealt with a tendency in my early twenties to binge/purge to fill my "loneliness holes" after I started a new job all alone in another state.

Learning not to deprive myself of favorite foods as a form of "punishment," I began to allow myself my very favorite things in normal amounts as often as I wanted them, but only eating enough to satisfy my hunger instead of binging. I learned to be satisfied with just a small amount, because I could always have more when I became hungry again.

I found when food lost its "forbidden-ness" for me, it also lost its allure for overindulging. Pausing and thinking what my body was really asking for also helped me to make much healthier food choices.

In this next section, we'll look at how food can indeed be our medicine. God gave us Whole Foods full of essential nutrients to heal our bodies. When man creates food in a factory that's sold in a box with a long shelf-life, it often contains chemicals and things we can't even pronounce that make us sick. These are things our body doesn't even recognize or know how to use. We need fresh foods with the vital nutrients God originally put into them to be our healthiest. The next section explains this in more detail.

Having worked in this area for many years, I know that this "F" can be a touchy subject for many. I only ask that you read the next F with an open mind, and ask God to speak His Truth to you in a way you can hear.

Then you can "take what you like, and leave the rest" from this, sweet sister.

PART 3

Healing Your Body

**When we are alive,
our bodies house the Lord Himself:**

Do you not know that you are God's temple and that
God's Spirit dwells in you? 1 Corinthians 3:16 (ESV)

**When we die,
our physical bodies return to where they came from: the earth.**

The Lord God formed man of the dust of the ground … Genesis 2:7a

For you were made from dust, and to dust you will return.
Genesis 3:19b

F5: FOOD

When I was diagnosed with breast cancer, I didn't know a lot about eating the way God intended for good health. I'd recently started to learn about a Whole Food way of eating that reminded me of foods we grew in our summer garden on the farm, but cooked in a new, healthier way. At the same time, information was starting to come out about the dangers of all the additives and chemicals in our food.

> I grew up on a beef farm in the Midwest, near the Mississippi River. The food we fed our livestock was heavily sprayed with herbicides and pesticides. Farmers routinely sprayed their crops to remove weeds and insects. It was the "modern way."
>
> I remember the awful smell whenever chemicals were stored in our barn, or sprayed on the crops. Playing in the grain bins where the harvested crops were stored made me itch, causing me to break out in horrible hives. But I never thought about what those chemicals were also doing to the inside of me, especially when I ate the food that had been sprayed.
>
> Seventeen years ago, when my surgeon looked at my pathology report, he asked me: "Where did you grow up?" When I answered, "On a farm in the Midwest," he replied: "I think the farm chemicals, the herbicides and pesticides, contributed to your tumors. If you also drank well water that came from springs that collected run-off from the fields, you took in even more toxic chemicals."

What an eye opener for me, but it did make sense. We didn't know these common farm chemicals could harm our health fifty years ago when I was a kid!

Thankfully we now know for certain that herbicides and pesticides are harmful to our body and our overall health. Many knowledgeable people along the walk were willing to help me learn what's true and what isn't about healthy eating. A basic summary of what we know about healthy eating follows. (For more information about healthy eating and a free Bible study on "Healthy Eating for All God's Children," see my website: www.HisCompleteTransformation.com .)

WHOLE FOOD: THE HEALTHIEST WAY TO EAT

As a Wellness Consultant for the last nineteen years, I've researched the impact numerous different eating plans have on our health. The underlying approach for every balanced and life-giving eating plan I've studied can be summed up in two simple words: Whole Food.

What exactly is Whole Food? In my work with women, I define Whole Food as *real food* in the form God created it, and unprocessed. You can cook Whole Food, or you can eat it raw. We generally grow up knowing which form of preparation (cooked, raw, or either way) is best for the foods we eat. You can also combine a variety of Whole Foods, which includes herbs and spices, in recipes to create delicious, healthy dishes for you and your family.

God knew that real food, His Whole Food, heals. He created it that way! Whole Food nourishes our bodies. It gives us energy that lasts, with no peaks and valleys. It keeps us healthy and feeling our best.

Our main objective should always be to eat Whole Foods the way God originally made them. I recommend you eat Whole Foods that are Organic whenever possible; but if you can't, be sure to wash conventionally grown (non-organic) produce especially well. You also will want to wash Organic produce to remove any bacteria or germs that come from being handled by others. (At the end of this section, there is a simple way to clean vegetables and fruits at home.)

When we say a Whole Food is also a clean food, this means it is a food that has few, if any, chemicals, preservatives, or other toxic substances we can't pronounce added to it. This is the healthiest type of food to eat. If a food is labeled Organic, no chemicals or toxic substances are used to grow or preserve it.

The beauty of this plan is it simplifies our choices, while giving us an immense variety of unaltered foods to choose from that fit our personal tastes. This approach is life-giving and helps prevent disease, as evidenced in numerous published studies.

Packaged food, on the other hand, can make us sick if we eat it frequently. Packaged food is not "alive," and it is missing many of the nutrients of Whole Foods. It depletes our body of health and lasting energy. It often makes us fat. Sadly, it is often "designed" to be addictive.

For your good health, and to prevent a cancer reoccurrence, avoid packaged food whenever possible. Choose live food, Whole Food, real food—God's Food! With a little more effort, knowledge, and commitment on your part, you will begin to choose Whole Food as close to the way God created it as possible. It will take planning, and it will take relying on God's continual help through His Holy Spirit that dwells within you.

His Spirit is an ever-present help in time of need. Keep this weapon close to your heart and foremost in your thoughts every moment of every day. It is His Spirit in us that allows us to resist temptation when we rely on His strength and not our own.

A cancer-preventing approach to eating is always based on Whole Foods, with the focus on vegetables and fruits. Why? Whole Food, or real food, is just that. It is complete. It is real. It is what God created to fuel our bodies, and keep us healthy. God did not make a donut tree, or a pizza roll bush. He made apple trees and bushes full of amazing berries. He made cows, not burgers loaded with fatty sauces served on white-bread buns. He made chickens, not chicken nuggets.

In other words, dear sisters, we can know God gave us Whole Foods for the health and nourishment of our human bodies.

THE CORNERSTONE OF A HEALTHY DIET: VEGETABLES AND FRUITS!

Vegetables and fruits are our primary source of the life-giving nutrients God gave us. We were designed to feel our best when we plan our meals around fresh or frozen vegetables and fruits, without anything added, unless it is another Whole Food.

Vegetables and fruits provide us with over 12,000 known phytochemicals. Phytochemicals are the chemical compounds in fruits and vegetables that supply us with the variety of the nutrients needed to keep our bodies healthy and free of disease. God clearly tells us in the first chapter of the Bible that fruits and vegetables are the mainstay of the food He created for us to eat:

> "Look! I have given you every seed-bearing plant throughout the earth and all the fruit trees for your food." Genesis 1:29

Research continues to pour in about the newly-discovered benefits of eating the way God intended for us to eat. One of the most powerful research statistics about how our food choices can help prevent cancer reoccurrences cannot be ignored:

"Eating five or more servings of fruits and vegetables per day and walking briskly for 30 minutes most days reduces the chance of reoccurrence in breast cancer survivors by 50 percent," states the American Institute for Cancer Research (AICR).

Five or more servings of fruits and vegetables should be our minimum daily goal, dear sisters.

Other important reasons to eat a diet rich in vegetables and fruit follow:

1. Non-starchy vegetables are a source of energy that will help stabilize blood sugar and insulin levels. This keeps our energy levels balanced, and our moods stable throughout the day. It also keeps harmful stress chemicals from forming as the body tries to balance itself after a sugary snack.

2. These same vegetables contain many of the vitamins, minerals, and antioxidants needed to produce healthy cells in our amazing bodies.

3. Starchy vegetables such as sweet potatoes, winter squash, and other types of potatoes are nutrient-dense, high-carbohydrate vegetables that can effectively meet energy needs while providing additional vitamins, minerals, and antioxidants we need for good health.

4. A diet rich in vegetables and fruits has been shown to lower LDL (harmful cholesterol) and prevent heart disease.

5. A diet rich in berries has been shown to reduce the negative effects of fat in the arteries after eating a high fat meal.

6. A diet rich in vegetables and fruits (nine to thirteen servings a day) has been shown to bring the body into a healthier, weight-balanced state.

7. A diet rich in vegetables and fruits (with ½ your plate made up of a variety of non-starchy vegetables; and free of harmful fats, sugars, and starches) has been shown to significantly reduce your risk of heart disease, cancer, diabetes, obesity, and more by 80%!

8. Vegetables and fruit are excellent sources of fiber. Fiber fills us up and helps stabilize our blood sugar; it also "cleans us out." Regular, healthy bowel movements are necessary to remove toxins and waste from our bodies, so they can't be re-absorbed. The fiber in fruits and vegetables literally act as little scrub brushes, removing harmful waste from our colons. We need a minimum of thirty to fifty grams of fiber per day to remain regular. People eating diets of nearly 100% plant foods consumed around one hundred grams of fiber a day. It's said in health circles open to talking about elimination that we should have a bowel movement after each meal. Certainly, with one hundred grams of fiber you would!

9. The phytonutrients in vegetables and fruits are amazing, further detoxifying our bodies of the harmful substances from polluted water and air. Cruciferous vegetables, like broccoli,

cabbage, kale, and cauliflower, are literally so powerful at detoxifying our bodies (and helping to prevent breast cancer) that they deserve a special mention. They contain a special protector, sulforaphane, that further protects us from a breast cancer reoccurrence. (ncbi.nlm.rih.gov)

10. This final reason trumps all others in my opinion: God tells us to in His Word! This verse bears repeating here: "Look! I have given you every seed-bearing plant throughout the earth and all the fruit trees for your food." Genesis 1:29

Let's take some time now to record our thoughts about what we've just read.

- What did you learn about the foods our Creator made for us to eat?
- What ways do you plan on modifying your diet to include more fruits and vegetables?
- If you are hesitant to add more fruits and veggies in your diet, or find it very difficult to do, you can refer to Resources at the end of this book.

★★★

When I went to Oasis of Hope hospital for alternative treatment before the mastectomy, we were served a "Gerson diet." A Gerson diet is based on frequently drinking freshly-made organic juices in combinations known for their healing properties. We were also served steamed vegetables and plain baked potatoes for dinner, but the focus was on drinking pure, organic juices to cleanse and nourish our bodies.

In the classes offered at the Hospital on juicing and eating Whole Foods, I learned the reason they highly recommended patients continue following this way of eating after leaving the hospital. When we are eating a wide variety of Whole Foods, with a focus on fruits and vegetables, we are causing our bodies to eliminate stored toxins. We are also giving our bodies "live" nutrients to begin to heal, an important step in our quest to become cancer-free. This is exactly what I wanted to do before more surgery.

I also received colonics to cleanse my colon, laetrile (a natural form of chemotherapy) through a chemo port, chelation therapy, heavy doses of Vitamin C, and other holistic treatments. Because I wanted to do my part in walking out my healing with the Lord's help, I fully participated in everything offered. Oasis was a Christ-focused hospital, and I trusted what the doctors recommended.

Dr. Contreras, M.D., head of the hospital in Mexico, came in to see me with the results of my lung x-ray (the most likely place the cancer would have spread, he believed). He offered me his recommendation: "There is no sign of cancer in your lungs. I would recommend you save the big guns—chemotherapy—for any possible reoccurrences. If you have the mastectomy when you get home, I believe you will be completely cured."

I returned home seventeen days later, ready to have surgery to remove any remaining tumors. After the mastectomy, my surgeon walked into my hospital room shaking his head in amazement. He said: "I don't quite understand what you did in Mexico, but those tumors I know I cut through were completely gone when you came back and had the mastectomy. Whatever you did worked!"

Dr. Contreras' words still ring true in my ears and my heart. Although the cells from tumors removed during my biopsy-turned-lumpectomy were dissolved and eliminated by the treatments I had at Oasis, my largest tumor, number thirteen—still intact and undiscovered by any tests—remained in the top quadrant of my left breast. My dense breast tissue kept this last tumor completely hidden until my left breast was removed during the mastectomy.

Dear sisters, only a mastectomy would have removed this last—and largest—tumor! God can and does work through our doctors who give us their best advice when they are guided by God.

***

While doing research for my own walk, I learned that breast cancer survivors who are focused on preventing a reoccurrence are taught to follow the same recommendations that are given for preventing breast cancer from occurring.

Those recommendations are:

- Maintain a healthy body weight.
- Get regular physical activity. Experts suggest walking briskly for at least 30 minutes most days. (See F6: Fitness for more information.)
- Consume a primarily plant-based diet.
- At least half of your plate should include non-starchy fruits and vegetables. Protein from animal sources, including fish, is limited to four ounces of clean protein (organic and/or grass fed, or wild caught if fish) one to two times a day.
- If you do drink, limit alcohol intake to one drink or less per day. New research indicates that more than four or five drinks (five ounces of wine or twelve ounces of beer) a week increases your chances of a breast cancer reoccurrence.
- For new mothers, breast feeding for more than six months is recommended. According to breastcancer.org, this is helpful because making milk limits the ability for breast cells "to misbehave." Women also tend to eat healthier while breastfeeding and have fewer menstrual cycles, resulting in lower estrogen levels–all things that reduce the risk of breast cancer.

Take a few moments now to record your thoughts on these suggestions, and what changes you want to make with your own approach to eating.

★★★

I'm often asked for specific examples of what I recommend women with breast cancer eat. The following lists give you some personal suggestions followed by my reasons.

TEN "FOODS" I WOULD GIVE UP COMPLETELY IF I HAD A SERIOUS ILLNESS AGAIN

1. Sugar in any form. Sugar feeds cancer cells. Cancer cells metabolize ("eat") sugar fifty times faster than healthy cells. [1] You do not want to provide fuel for the cancer cells.

2. White flour, white pasta, white rice, or any other white starch. White starches are metabolized just like sugar in the body.

3. Dairy, including cheese, milk, cream, yogurt, ice cream, etc., even low fat or organic. Dairy produces mucous which is not a good environment for preventing or healing cancer.

4. All meat, except for wild caught fish, organic/free range eggs, and maybe wild meat (like elk or buffalo) occasionally. I would seriously consider following a Vegan diet, which means I would eat no animal products whatsoever. I began to follow this type of diet during my stay at Oasis Hospital. When I came home, I continued eating Vegan during treatment and recovery. Meat consumption remains controversial, dear sisters, with no clear science supporting it, and research is now showing meat consumption is harmful for breast cancer patients.[2] Humans were originally created to eat only plant foods, but God included meat in their diets after the flood. At the very least, I would minimize meat consumption after diagnosis and during treatment.

5. All fats but those listed on the next page. Toxins are stored in unclean fats.

6. All GMO (genetically modified organism) foods. GMO foods are foods that have been genetically altered by man to be different than the perfect way God created them.

7. Soy, unless it is organic. Only organic soy is not genetically altered or heavily sprayed with harmful chemicals. Please note: soy consumption can also be controversial, but one serving a day of organic soy is what I was allowed by my nutritionally-astute oncologist.

8. Any fruit or vegetable from Chile or Mexico that is not organic, due to their heavy use of pesticides, including several pesticides not allowed in the U.S.

9. Alcohol in any form, including red wine. Alcohol has been linked to an increased risk of breast cancer in numerous studies. (If you enjoy a glass of red wine several times a week, you can have wine or the occasional mixed drink again when you've been cancer-free for at least a year.)

10. All snack foods, even organic versions, like potato chips, corn chips, candy, etc. Healthier choices, like fresh fruits and vegetables, are your best options because they are full of the nutrients God put in them. So are small quantities of walnuts and almonds, air popped popcorn, and unsweetened dried fruit.

IF I CAN'T EAT THOSE FOODS, WHAT CAN I EAT? PERHAPS THE 10 BEST FOODS FOR YOU

1. Organic vegetables and fruits contain antioxidants, minerals, and fiber.

2. Unsalted raw or lightly roasted nuts and seeds contain Omega 3 oils, fiber, and protein.

3. Organic beans contain protein and fiber, and they are filling. Canned beans are okay if you rinse them off first.

4. Whole grain or short grain organic brown rice and other whole grains contain fiber, carbohydrates, and some protein.

5. Filtered water should be your beverage of choice. Water flushes your body, and carbon filtered water removes the chlorine and toxic minerals while retaining the good minerals.

6. Organic green tea contains more antioxidants and less caffeine than coffee or black tea.

7. Wild caught fish, especially salmon and Mahi-Mahi, are excellent sources of protein and Omega 3 oils. Avoid farmed fish of any kind.

8. Raw honey, preferably locally harvested, can be medicinal. Only a teaspoon is needed for sweetness.
9. Organic or cage-free eggs contain protein and choline.
10. Small amounts (1 T. or less) of coconut or avocado oil for cooking, cold-pressed olive oil for salads, and organic butter or ghee are healthy fats that are very satisfying.

(More examples of healthy Whole Foods to eat are available for free on my website: www.HisCompleteTransformation.com.)

As we wrap up F5: Food, I would like to leave you with these three take-away tips:

- You cannot eat too many unsweetened vegetables, unless you smother them in rich sauces or deep fat fry them. For optimal health, and for rebuilding your body after cancer, eat at least six servings of vegetables a day. Two to three fruits a day is plenty; berries are the most nutritionally dense choice. Vegetables are powerhouses for helping rebuild your body after surgery and treatment.

- The more you focus on eating vegetables, the easier it becomes to lose any excess weight you've gained from treatment or forced inactivity from surgery. You are also providing a gentle cleanse for your body to rid itself of toxins that have accumulated over the years, and may have contributed to your cancer in the first place.

- Consider juicing organic fruits and vegetables. If you cannot juice, then take a clean, high quality, well researched, Whole Food supplement made only from fruits and vegetables. (See Resources for suggestions.) Better yet, do both.

WISDOM FROM THE WORD

God places a high value on the bodies He gave us:

> Or do you not know that your body is a temple of the Holy Spirit within you, whom you have from God? You are not your own, for you were bought with a price. So glorify God in your body. 1 Corinthians 6:19-20 (ESV)

> If you want to know what God wants you to do, ask Him, and He will gladly tell you, for He is always ready to give a bountiful supply of wisdom to all who ask Him; He will not resent it. But when you ask Him, be sure that you really expect Him to tell you, for a doubtful mind will be as unsettled as a wave of the sea that is driven and tossed by the wind; and every decision you then make will be uncertain, as you turn first this way and then that. If you don't ask with faith, don't expect the Lord to give you any solid answer. James 1:5-8 (TLB)

> Trust God from the bottom of your heart; don't try to figure out everything on your own. Listen for God's voice in everything you do, everywhere you go; He's the one who will keep you on track. Don't assume that you know it all. Run to God! Run from evil! Your body will glow with health, your very bones will vibrate with life! Proverbs 3:5-8 (MSG)

Keep in mind this already quoted Scripture concerning God's advice to us in Genesis 1:29. Like every Word from God in the Bible, it has stood the test of time!

> Then God said, "Look! I have given you every seed-bearing plant throughout the earth and all the fruit trees for your food."

God bless you, dear sisters!

A SIMPLE VINEGAR WASH FOR VEGETABLES AND FRUITS

A study published in 2003 in the "Journal of Food Protection" found that washing apples with a vinegar and water solution reduced salmonella on the outer skin significantly more than washing with water alone. According to Jack Bishop, editor of the magazine Cooks Illustrated, vinegar killed approximately 98 percent of bacteria on the surface of fresh fruits and vegetables during a similar experiment. (Source: www.livestrong.com)

To make your own wash, combine one-part white distilled vinegar with three-parts clean water. Put the mixture in a clean spray bottle. Leaving the skin intact, spray the unpeeled vegetable or fruit all over, and then use your clean hands to lightly scrub the entire outside. Rinse well under running water to remove the vinegar. You can also use a vegetable scrub brush for this purpose if you like. (I use the scrub brush for potatoes, for example.) Put the scrub brush in the dishwasher to sanitize it for your next use.

If an item is smaller, like greens, berries, and grapes, make a simple vinegar wash and let them soak for several minutes. I prefer to rinse berries and grapes under the sprayer from my kitchen faucet before and after soaking them. (Even Organic varieties have dirt on them.)

Dear sisters, I have written a free Bible Study about Healthy Eating, where I go into more detail about healthy foods we can eat, complete with an example of a "Healthy Plate," and a list of nutritious foods to choose from. By choosing healthy food ingredients, you can make a huge variety of delicious food. (See Resources.)

Take some time now to look back over any points that aren't clear to you, or that you want to learn more about. I recommend you either put a star beside them in your book, or list them in your Journal now.

When you are done journaling your thoughts about F5: Food, dear sisters, we will "move" together into F6: Fitness. This section will look at the importance of moving our bodies more, and the many benefits of being fit as part of our healing and cancer prevention walk.

F6: FITNESS

Fitness is defined as taking care of our bodies so we're able to move to the best of our ability. It's having strength, health, and a zest for life. When we are fit, we can do what we need to do without struggle or pain.

Think back to when you were a child, especially if you grew up in a smaller town or on a farm. For most of us older than thirty, we played outside at recess, walked to school, or rode our bikes. We couldn't wait to play outside again after school. Our natural tendency was to be active, and we wanted to do anything that didn't involve sitting at a school desk any longer than we had to. Movement was fun, and often necessary.

What happened to that desire to move our bodies in fun ways? Is it our fascination today with TVs, computers, gaming, or cell phones that keeps us incessantly busy, but not physically active? Or is it a job where we must sit all day? Could it also be thinking we just don't have time for fitness with everything else we must do?

If we are being honest, every one of us has gone through phases in our life where we just didn't move as much as we used to or need to. The less we move, sweet sisters, the harder it gets to be active. We also get out of the daily routine of exercising.

As a result, back pain starts, our muscles get weak or tight from not being used, weight creeps on, even laziness sets in. We find we just don't have the energy to move, forgetting that moderate exercise will give us more energy.

I understand this, dear sisters. I go through periods of getting out of my exercise routine too. I find it's so easy to not exercise if I don't make daily movement a high priority.

As I edit the first draft of this chapter, I realize I have fallen off the fitness wagon. I sit at the computer or on my loveseat, working on this book, for much of the day. I find excuses not to take a daily brisk walk in this heat. A day leads to a week, and soon it is months of more inactivity than I am used to.

This chapter is my own wake-up call. I see the results on the scale, in how I feel, and how my clothes no longer fit. After "muttering" about it for days, I reopen an email for this chapter, and reread the following lead sentence, mentioned previously under F5:

"Eating five or more servings of fruits and vegetables per day and walking briskly for thirty minutes most days reduces the chance of reoccurrence in breast cancer survivors by 50 percent."

Thinking this sounded too simple to be true, I contacted the author by email, asking her the source of this research. She told me that this important fact is based on gold standard research, not the latest internet buzz on health. It is based on solid science, dear sisters.

I've spent the last twenty years or so emphasizing the need to eat more than five servings of fruits and vegetables in my business. But I'd never seen it linked so directly to fitness before! It was a wake-up call for me to stop "muttering" about it and start moving.

God then gave me a prompting I had been resisting for years, but could no longer ignore. My husband and a friend got together at a neighborhood gathering and planned a way to slowly start me on a weight-lifting program to help my back pain, not to mention my fear of lifting anything heavier than five pounds.

Normally, I would have protested, found excuses, or simply refused to do it. I could have justified being angry because I hadn't been consulted. But since I'd been thinking about how to get started lifting light weights, I chose to believe God had given me a way to get started.

Now it was up to me to take action. I had to start doing my part to walk out God's healing for me again.

Oh, sweet sisters, we all fall off the wagon. We must pick ourselves up and get back on an exercise program. I know whether it's our first time, or our hundredth, every one of us can return to doing the right thing for our health because God is here to help us!

FITNESS AND PREVENTION

We just talked about the benefits of eating fruits and vegetables, in F5: Food. It is well worth mentioning again the combined value of walking briskly for thirty minutes most days, and eating at least five servings of vegetables and fruits a day to prevent a reoccurrence of breast cancer. The 50% reduction in the rate of reoccurrences when we do both is significant!

Exercise is also a wonderful stress reduction tool. Many studies link stress to breast cancer occurrences, most notably Dr. Susan Silberstein's report on beatcancer.org (see Resources), and this is one way we can "work off" our stress in a healthy way.

- Journal your thoughts about what you've just learned about the preventative benefits of exercising.

WE ARE CREATED TO MOVE

God created our bodies to move. He gave us the ability to walk, to move our arms, to pick up a child, to carry a grocery bag, or take care of our homes.

Biblical references to the word exercise or movement use the word very differently than we do today. There is very little direct mention of specifically exercising our bodies. The daily chores of life required people in Biblical times to be active as part of their lifestyle. Perhaps the Kings and other royalty were less active because they didn't do any physical labor, but most of the people needed to walk places and be physically active just to survive.

In the New Testament, we find Jesus walking from one place to the next, often using this time to teach His disciples. His exercise was natural; it was a part of His daily routine. With all the conveniences of modern life, it's easy to observe how we don't need to do as much physical work or activity as previous generations. As a result, we must find ways to move more and schedule times to be active each day.

Caring for our bodies is an act of worship and stewardship, dear sisters. Take some time now to give this some prayerful thought and consideration. Write out your thoughts in your Journal. Ask yourself:

- Am I willing to focus on being fit by moving more?
- If not, what is holding me back?

WHAT IS THE BEST EXERCISE FOR YOU?

You've probably heard this answer before: "The best exercise is the one you will do."

Makes sense, doesn't it? You can join the fanciest gym, but if you won't go, the membership does you no good. Take some time now to journal about these questions to help you get started:

- To discover what exercise you'd enjoy doing, answer these questions: Did you play a sport in school, or informally in the neighborhood? Did you enjoy skating, hiking up hills or mountains, taking PE classes, dancing, or riding your bike? If none of these apply to you, consider walking. As a kid, I loved walking in the pasture to herd the cows back to the barn for the late afternoon milking. Walking or jogging have always been my favorite forms of exercise.

- Is there an exercise program you were doing before the diagnosis that you'd like to do again?
- Would you like to try something new you just haven't made time for before?

If you don't already have a good exercise routine you do regularly, I would suggest you try walking. Walking on level, smooth surfaces is usually something most people can safely do without injury. After getting the okay from your doctor, begin with walking to your mailbox, or the end of your block, if you aren't usually active. If you can do more, try for a mile your first day, or seven minutes each direction if you don't know the distance. You can always add more distance or time later.

Start slowly and work up. Don't attempt to do more than what you're used to doing if it's a new activity for you, and do not start out walking on a long or steep trail. Give your body a chance to adjust so you don't overdo it and want to quit. Fitness is something we work toward, dear sisters; it's not an overnight accomplishment. Injury derails our best intentions!

I recently found out that my smart phone has a free app on it that tracks my steps each day, like a basic pedometer. I love it! I often get to the end of the day, and notice that moving a little more will help me reach my desired daily number of steps. I usually decide to take the trash out, walk outside for a few minutes, or pick up the house. Keeping track of my steps motivates me and helps me stay active.

You can also try exercise shows on TV or YouTube. Buy a video if that works better for you. Experiment, try different things. Have fun with it! Dance around the house! Bodies that move are a gift. Just ask anyone who has trouble moving.

There's a variety of fun and interesting ways to be active with your family and friends, or on your own: biking, skating, skiing, hiking, raking the yard, cleaning the house (well, maybe not fun—but it can be good exercise if you clean vigorously), basketball, tennis, swimming, racquetball, kicking a ball around, water classes, playing tag with your kids, etc. Mix it up, if you prefer variety. And let's not forget walking a dog can be a great motivator, if the dog will walk at a steady and continuous pace.

Here's a fun fact to know: consistent movement affects our emotions in a positive way. If I am worried or angry about something, I can remove myself from the situation and take a walk around the block or in the woods. Or I can dig in the yard, clean vigorously, sweep the decks, or anything that requires me to move my body with energy for a continuous amount of time.

Getting outside is always a plus for me. I love the sunshine, fresh air, or cool rain. The movement gets my blood flowing in a positive way; and I often pray while I walk, which gives me a fresh and better perspective on things. Try it; it really works!

Look back now at the list of ways to move your body that are mentioned above. Check off or jot down at least two or three you would like to try or add to your daily routine. Then commit to trying one for at least a week. Don't make it a race or exceed your limits if it is a new activity, or if you are not currently active.

Thirty minutes a day, five or six days a week, is what you are striving for, but you can start with what you can do. Your doctor will be able to tell you when he or she thinks you are ready to start or resume exercising.

If you find that longer blocks of time are a challenge, try working up to exercising for (3) 10-minute periods a day. Be flexible, and do what works for you. You will reap numerous benefits from your efforts, I promise, if you will give it time.

Virtually everyone I've coached or worked with already knows that we need to incorporate some sort of exercise or consistent movement into our daily lives to feel and look better. But knowledge doesn't translate into action unless you purposefully decide to exercise.

These four steps will help you get started:

1. Exercise requires a plan to make it happen! Ask yourself:
    *   **What** am I going to do? Am I going to walk, go to a class, use a treadmill or bike at home, or something else? Choose one now.

- **When** am I going to do it? Am I going to exercise first thing in the morning, after work, during lunch hour, or at another time? Be specific.
- **Where** am I going to do it? Am I going to exercise at home, in my neighborhood, at a gym, or drive to a trail or park? Pick a place.

2. Exercise requires some preparation by you before it can happen:
   - You must schedule it. It needs to be on your calendar for it to happen.
   - You must join a gym, sign up for a class, plan a route, etc.
   - You must purchase shoes, equipment, or whatever else you need that you don't already have.

3. Exercise requires a commitment to your plan of action.

4. Finally, exercise requires getting started: prepacking your gym bag or laying out your walking or running clothes the night before, taking that first step out the door, showing up for class, getting into the pool, or climbing on the treadmill. As the Nike slogan says: "Just do it!"

5. Finally, write out your plan. Post it somewhere where you can see it every morning. It will remind you of your intention to move more.

If you work full time, planned breaks are opportunities to get more movement into your day. One of our sons works on the phone in a high stress job every day. He and a co-worker set their watches to get up and walk around the building every hour, trying hard to stick with their plan. He tells me it's a great stress reducer and refresher, too!

It's been my experience that most people enjoy exercising after they do it consistently for three weeks or longer.

WISDOM FROM THE WORD

Sweet sisters, here are Scriptures to stand on when you are planning and doing your exercise routine. Please remember to start as slow as you need to, and build up from there. It is good to push ourselves a little, but don't overdo it. Your body is healing, and you are doing this out of love for the body God has given you, not punishment. Be gentle, yet firm, with yourself.

When I was recovering from major surgery, many simple things, such as getting out of bed and getting dressed, took such effort! These verses gave me great encouragement:

> For I can do everything through Christ, who gives me strength. Philippians 4:13

> She girds herself with strength and makes her arms strong. Proverbs 31:17 (NASB)

Know this, sweet sisters: whatever your age or exercise level, God promises to give us strength when we depend on Him:

> He gives power to the weak and strength to the powerless. Even youths will become weak and tired, and young men will fall in exhaustion. But those who trust in the Lord will find new strength. They will soar high on wings like eagles. They will run and not grow weary. They will walk and not faint. Isaiah 40:29-31

It's important to include strength training as part of your fitness program. There is solid evidence that weight training with even light weights (start with two, three, or five pounds) will benefit your bone strength. Free weights, stretch bands, kettle bells, or bodyweight exercises like push-ups all help.

If you've not done strength training before, I would wait until your doctor says it's okay to exercise, and then work with a trainer or someone who can teach you proper form. This will help prevent injuries. Look for a trainer who has worked with breast cancer patients before.

In closing, dear sisters, you can find strength in knowing that God wants each of us to live the life He created for us to live—a life that is free, full, and abundant.

★★★

Write your thoughts about exercising in your Journal.

- Write out how you intend to include this health promoting activity in your daily life.
- If you don't want to start moving more in planned and consistent ways, journal about your reasons for not exercising. Getting that out in the open (again for your eyes only, unless you choose to share your thoughts) can also help you make healthy changes in your lifestyle.
- What will you do this week? Write your plan of action in your Journal, and schedule it on your calendar now.

SURRENDERING PRAYER:

Oh, Heavenly Father, I humbly come before You in thanksgiving and praise for who You are, the living God! I promise You that I want my body to be a living sacrifice before You, the kind You will find acceptable. I want my daily life to be an act of worship to You, Lord, and I lean on the strength of Your Spirit to help me do this. Guide me to do what is pleasing in Your sight. Your will be done, not mine, oh Lord. In Jesus' name, Amen.

F7: FUN

When I sat down to write about Fun, I confess I really didn't know what to say. Granted, I'd learned the importance of having fun along the walk, yet I couldn't immediately describe it.

It took walking beside (and sometimes chasing down!) a delightful woman named Mary Lou in my *"Thriving in God's Love"* cancer support group at our church to add the seventh F. Mary Lou is committed to having fun in her life, at greater levels of enjoyment and laughter than most "well" people I know.

> *Four years earlier when Mary Lou's doctor told her she had Stage IV ovarian cancer with only a few months to live, Mary Lou decided to remain fully involved in living her life in all the ways that mattered to her. She stood on the firm foundation of her Christian faith for the strength to do this, dear sisters, despite what her doctors told her.*
>
> *Although Mary Lou didn't talk much about the specifics of her cancer when I met her several years later, I learned her cancer had spread to other parts of her body. It was obvious she wasn't given a medical reason to be full of joy, but she continued showing up for life each day with obvious joy in her heart.*
>
> *Her support group of other retired couples and friends who get together several times a week keeps her engaged. She has no time for self-pity, but she has all the time in the world to say an encouraging word to everyone she meets, and to share in a good laugh about something.*

Her young grandson recently died from diabetes, leaving the family in shock and pain. Mary Lou's unshakable faith in Jesus and His promise of eternal life have helped keep Mary Lou alive during this stressful and tragic time. She takes comfort in knowing she is going to Heaven whenever she dies, and she will see her grandson again. This solid hope gives her great peace.

Sweet sisters, after my diagnosis and treatment, I had to relearn the importance of having fun on a regular basis. I found it was essential to my own sense of well-being in my body, soul, and spirit. I discovered fun is more than just enjoyment of something for me. Fun often involves laughter, at least one other person whose company I enjoy, and usually seeing or doing something new. "Play" frequently factors in.

I find the more childlike I can become on a regular basis, the more fun I have. I think my sons are hilarious, and they have always found me funny. I'm glad, because not everyone else gets my sense of humor! One son nearly makes me roll on the floor laughing. The other son, while also very funny, often provides me with the best talks, another form of fun for me.

Talk about a double blessing!

I have friends who are funny, and they can be lighthearted, despite chronic illnesses and other problems in their lives. Being with them always makes me laugh and feel good. Surely this must be healing!

I also find animals very funny. Perhaps it's growing up on a farm with everything from cats to cows to goats that makes me think about what they might say if they could talk. It was my way of amusing myself, I guess. I'm certain I couldn't print some of what our demanding old cat was saying nearly every moment in his older days, but the rest of his antics as a younger cat always made me laugh. Our puppy is hilarious naturally (when she isn't eating something she's not supposed to eat!), and the many shelter kittens we foster-cared were so entertaining with their natural antics! If you have pets, you probably know what I mean.

For healing, dear sisters, we each need to be aware of what

specifically brings us joy. Each person has "unique to her" things that bring her happiness, and these are very important for healing.

Several things that bring me joy include: walking outside in new locations, looking at flowers, reading, meaningful conversations with friends or just visiting (not gossiping), eating good food, sipping a great glass of iced tea or iced coffee, observing pretty colors in nature, watching animals, or seeing animals I've not seen before. I also like a quiet house to myself. Being by myself in complete quiet when I've been especially busy rejuvenates me.

As I walk out this part of healing, I've started paying more attention to what brings me joy. How about you? Pause now and ask yourself:

- What brings me joy?
- What can I do today that would bring me pleasure and refresh me?

I can also incorporate more joy in my life by observing a Sabbath day each week, which is a day of rest from work and continual striving to get things done.

This is how that looks for me: I usually attend a Saturday evening church service at my Christian church. Then on Sunday, my husband and I take our dog for a long walk somewhere we enjoy. We often end the walk by eating breakfast out, and then coming home to do nothing that resembles work. I don't write (only journaling for myself), but I do read, have my devotions and quiet time with God in His Word, nap if I want, and usually have little contact with others outside our family. As an introvert, I seem to need this quiet time, but you might prefer to spend time with others you care about—family, friends, neighbors, etc.

The many gifts of this time include feeling rested and refreshed. I've learned the world keeps on turning without me actively doing "necessary" things every day. Unlike the Jewish people of the Old Testament, I do not have stringent laws making it a challenge for me to "correctly" observe the Sabbath. Instead, I take a day of rest, much like the Lord did during creation and recommends in the third commandment:

> Remember to observe the Sabbath day by keeping it holy. Exodus 20:8

I've also come to notice something else. Not only did God rest from His work, but He always took time to enjoy the fruits of His labor. On my Sabbath, I can enjoy what God has made, and what He has given me. This leaves the field wide open for opportunities to enjoy what brings me joy.

I hope it does the same for you, sweet sister! As we learn to take better care of ourselves after breast cancer, we will come to understand that joy and gratitude are healing states of mind. As you walk out your own healing, make a point of including something of joy in each day.

BENEFITS OF LAUGHTER

Why is it important to laugh? Science (see www.mayoclinic.com) has discovered that laughter is a potent stress reliever for the following reasons:

- Laughter helps us breathe more deeply to oxygenate our blood.
- Laughter causes our bodies to release endorphins, our own natural pain killers, and we feel better.
- Our bodies produce more immune cells, helping to fight off cancer growth.
- Our lungs and heart are stimulated in a healthy way.
- Our pulse slows, our blood pressure goes down, and our muscles relax after a good laugh, lessening our pain levels.
- We burn more calories when we laugh!

Dr. Francisco Contreras, M.D., the cancer specialist I consulted with at Oasis of Hope Hospital in Tijuana, says: "One bout of anger will diminish the efficiency of your immune system for six hours, but one good laugh will increase the efficiency of your immune systems for 24 hours."

In the forward to Charles and Frances Hunter's book <u>Healing through Humor</u>, Dr. Contreras goes on to say: *"Science has definitely confirmed the potent healing factor of laughter. Whether studies were conducted in Japan[3] or Loma Linda, California[4], objective results indicate that patients who experience laughter receive a boost to their immune system as measured in the elevation of natural killer cell activity and immune-globulin"* (a complex group of proteins that serve as antibodies in your immune system).

"There are so many objective clinical trials that support the healing power of humor that it surprises me that few doctors take advantage of this 'medication.'"

Once again, science has finally proven what God told us years ago in His word:

A cheerful heart is good medicine ... Proverbs 17:22

Now, consider this Scripture:

Your hands made me and formed me; give me understanding to learn Your commands. Psalm 119:73 (NIV)

Answer these questions in your Journal now, dear sister, for a deeper grasp of what this passage means to you about the importance of fun, relaxation, and rest:

- What would be the benefit for us if we asked God for more understanding about His commands?
- What did you just learn about His commands that you might not have known before?

I'd like to close this section on Fun with the testimony Mary Lou had written a few months before I met her:

MARY LOU'S STORY

I am so honored to give a testimony about our Heavenly Father's power to heal. On September 19th, 2016, I found out I was in my second remission. You know how our Jesus can take a horrible sinful life and turn it into something beautiful? Well, I am here to tell you, He can do the same with a death-threatening illness. I know He has done this for me, and He continues to bless me. I have been kept pain-free, which is a miracle for someone with a serious cancer.

My own journey started on November 3rd, 2013. Blessing #1 appeared at my hospital room door. After seeing the look on the doctor's face, I realized there was no good news to come. I had Stage IV ovarian cancer with three months to live. The doctor said I should get my affairs in order. I know that might have sounded harsh, but the kind, sweet way she told me was Blessing #1. She sat on the bed and held my hand with tears in her eyes and related to me how sorry she was. This caring doctor brought comfort and peace into a difficult situation.

Blessing #2 was already by my side—my husband, daughter, and dear friends.

One hour later Blessing #3 appeared at the door, my cancer doctor. I'd been seeing him for two years while he monitored a bone cancer possibility that never materialized. Praise God! He said he thought he could help me again if I was willing to try some harsh chemotherapy treatments.

Blessing #4, the most precious of all, started to take hold of me. I realized how much my Jesus loved me! He has blessed me with a beautiful church family and friends who have constantly prayed for my health and healing.

Jesus also sent me a precious Stephens Minister, Annie, who is now one of my dearest friends. She has blessed me beyond measure. With her help, I began to see Jesus as my great Physician, and my cancer doctor as Jesus' assistant.

Even if Jesus hadn't chosen to heal me, I believe I am still in a "win-win situation." You see, Jesus died on the cross for my sins, and I have accepted His free gift of salvation. I don't know what He has planned for my earthly life in the future, but what I do know is this: I will spend eternity with Him, joining my loved ones and friends who also believe in Him.

Thank you for allowing me to share the incredible way Jesus healed my life. I pray I can continue to live a life that brings Him the glory.

I dedicate this chapter to Mary Lou, who remained full of His joy as this book was initially submitted. Praise God!

CONCLUSION

As we wrap up our time together, dear sisters, I would like to ask you the most important question I believe you will ever answer. My hope for you is that you will give your response serious prayer and consideration. Cancer was a wake-up call for me—really driving home the fact that my earthly life would end one day—and I didn't know when that would be. This gave me the opportunity to respond to this question when I heard it asked:

WHERE DO YOU WANT TO SPEND ETERNITY?

I considered this the most important question for me to answer when I was diagnosed with breast cancer for this reason: when we die, our spirit—the part of us that is eternal—must continue to exist somewhere. We generally call this place "eternity," which is vague as to its location, but clear in its definition: Eternity is the place that exists forever; it is the place that will never go away or be destroyed.

Sweet sisters, I believe we get to choose where we will spend eternity. This choice is a direct result of the free will that God, in His great love, gives each of us, and it requires us to choose what I call our "final destination."

> *Since breast cancer, whenever I fly, the announcement of our*
> *"final destination" always strikes me as a very important*
> *one. It's intended to make sure if we are planning to go to a*

certain place, we are on a plane that's ultimately bound for that destination before we even take off.

The announcement is our last call to de-board if we've accidentally chosen, whether by mistake or confusion, to get on the wrong flight. Once the doors close, and we are on our way, it's too late. We cannot change our mind. Our "final destination" is inevitable.

Cancer forced me to think very seriously about where the final destination of my life would actually be. When faced with a disease I knew I might die from, I had a deep longing to know with certainty where I would spend eternity.

When I looked at my choices, only one destination became vital to my peace of mind. I did not want to be separated from God.

You know my back story. You know I was sampling from a smorgasbord of possibilities about God and eternity. When I came to understand this dabbling would put me on a "plane" bound for a place I did not want to go, dear sisters, it became clear to me that I needed to **choose** the destination I wanted, now.

I wanted to be in Heaven. I wanted to spend eternity in God's holy presence. The other option, eternal separation from God, which the Bible defines as Hell, was clearly not where I wanted to spend eternity.

I couldn't buy a ticket to Heaven, of course, or earn it with good deeds, but I could answer a call I'd been sensing in my heart during my quieter moments. I could say "Yes" to Jesus gently knocking at the door to my heart while He was saying:

> "Look! I have been standing at the door, and I am constantly knocking. If anyone hears Me calling him and opens the door, I will come in and fellowship with him and he with Me." Revelation 3:20 (TLB)

Dear sisters, I decided to open the door of my heart, and begin to know God through His Son, Jesus Christ. I fully accepted Jesus as my

Lord and Savior through repentance and full-immersion baptism. This type of baptism is not required for salvation, dear sisters, but it is the way Jesus Himself was baptized. It was a very important step for me.

Sometimes we resist Jesus until our deathbed, when I believe His consistent knocking and calling out to us gets the loudest. God does not desire that anyone would be "destroyed" (go to a place of eternal separation from God), but that all would live. He wants us to be with Him for eternity:

> He does not want anyone to be destroyed, but wants everyone to repent. (2 Peter 3:9b)

How amazing is His great love for us!

If you, too, sweet sister, want to accept His gracious offer of living forever in His presence with "no more sorrow and no more pain," which the Bible defines as Heaven, you can pray aloud this heartfelt prayer now:

> *Oh, Lord, I am opening the door to my heart for You right now. I invite You into my life. Thank You for dying on the cross for my sins, and giving me eternal life. I need You, Lord Jesus. I want to know Your love for me; I want to receive You as my Lord and Savior. Come in now, please. Amen.*

This simple prayer fulfills what Jesus Himself said about salvation:

> "I am the way, the truth and the life. No one can come to the Father except through Me." John 14:6

It also accomplishes what the Apostle Paul tells us about salvation:

> There is salvation in no one else! God has given no other name under Heaven by which we must be saved. Acts 3:12

If you have not made your own personal decision about where you will spend eternity, I suggest you give this some serious prayer and consideration. Once you decide, make the commitment out loud, as well as in your heart. Both are very important.

I recommend you become involved in a Bible-based Christian church. Get to know God through His Son Jesus by reading His Word, and spending time with Him. Prayer and meditation on Scripture are vital to this process.

Dear sisters, in closing, I want to repeat that this is the most important question you will ever answer. With your answer, you choose where you will spend eternity. If you say "Yes" to Jesus' invitation to be with Him in Heaven, you will be saying "Yes" to a forever friend who will love you without fail. Maybe you've never had that in your life; but with God, you can count on His love that "endures forever."

I've come to realize that it doesn't get any better than this. I have finally found the One who will never leave me or give up on me. Dear sister, God never wants any of us to have cancer, nor does He ever cause it. Satan causes all evil, not God. I can have complete peace, knowing this is clearly the "good" (Romans 8:28) that God worked together for me during my walk with breast cancer.

> When I was brought low, He saved me. Psalm 116:6
> (NIV)

I praise Your Holy Name, Lord Jesus!

As we close our time together, my prayer is that my experience, strength, and hope from my own breast cancer walk will shine a Light on your own walk. May God bless you richly with His Shalom blessing of peace, wholeness, and completeness in this life and the next, dear sister.

Always remember, dear sisters, it is God's love that heals us for all eternity.

I'll leave you with several lines from one of my favorite songs of praise, *"My Story."* God's love for us never gives up, dear sisters, and the real Hope we can have in Him won't let go.

If I told you my story
You would hear hope that wouldn't let go...
You would hear love that never gave up.

If I should speak then let it be ...
Of the Kindness of Jesus that draws me in

To tell you my story is to tell of Him.
This is my story, this is my song, praising my Savior all the day long.

Dear sister, if you found this book helpful, I encourage you to order another sister her own copy. By keeping your own copy, you will want to refer to it as you continue to walk out your own healing. A diagnosis of cancer usually gives us sofa or bed time, whether we want it or not. Encouraging and helpful books, such as this one, are a good way to pass the time of recovery in an impactful way.

ABOUT THE AUTHOR

Suzanne Bonner grew up in a small farm town in the Midwest, enjoyed big city life as a young, married woman, and then returned near where both families lived before her parents died.

When Suzanne had breast cancer, her favorite "nurse" during her recovery had four paws, a tail, and a lovely purr. Now she enjoys the family dog, but remains grateful for the numerous healing hours spent with a faithful cat who excelled in both restorative rest and loyal support.

She lives with her husband in Flagstaff, AZ, an area they chose as a great place to raise their sons. Their sons are now twenty-three and twenty-five, and currently live in Arizona. Suzanne teaches Bible studies at her local church, and is honored to walk with other breast cancer survivors through her *Thriving in God's Love* small groups and online classes.

Suzanne loves to walk, especially in new areas. She also loves observing God's beautiful flowers, eating delicious and healthy foods, and finishing every meal with dark chocolate with almonds! Her dream as a young girl was to be a teacher, and one day write a book. Her mother's secret dream, verbalized only once, was for Suzanne to be a missionary. Perhaps this book is Suzanne's way to do both by sharing God's Word with others in large and small groups, wherever God takes her.

Any hope and healing these words offer for others, dear sisters, comes from God and His loving kindness for each of us. To Him be the glory!

BIBLE TRANSLATIONS USED

I've noted the Bible Translations used for Scriptures in the text after every Scripture. When there is no Translation noted, then I've used the New Living Translation (NLT) published by the Tyndale House Foundation.

The Translations I've used are available on www.BibleGateway.com:

AMP: Amplified Bible
AMPC: Classic Edition
ESV: English Standard Version
KJV: King James Version
KJ21: 21st Century King James Version
MEV: Modern English Version
MSG: The Message
NASB: New American Standard Bible
NCV: New Century Version
NIV: New International Version
NKJV: New King James Version
NLT: New Living Translation
TLB: Living Bible
VOICE: The Voice

BIBLIOGRAPHY

F5: Food

[1] Warburg, *The Metabolism of Tumors* (London: Constable, 1930); O. Warburg, "On the Origin of Cancer Cells," *Science* 123, no. 3191 (February 24, 1956): 309-14.

[2] J.R. Hebert, T.G. Hurley, and Y. Ma, "The Effect of Dietary Exposures on Recurrence and Mortality in Early State Breast Cancer," *Breast Cancer Research and Treatment 51, no. 1* (September 1998): 17-28.

F7: Fun

[3] Takahashi, M. Iwase, et al, "The elevation of natural killer cell activity induced by laughter in a crossover study," International Journal of Molecular Medicine,[5] December 2001, 8(6):645-650.

[4] L.S. Berk, D.L. Felten, et al, "Modulation of neuroimmune parameters during the eustress or humor-associated mirthful laughter," Alternative Therapies in Health and Medicine, March 2001, 7(2):62-72, 74-76.

RESOURCES

Trusted resources are very helpful when faced with breast cancer. To give you the most current information on each Resource I personally use for my own health and well-being, I refer you to my website: www. HisCompleteTransformation.com. You will also find a free *"Healthy Eating for All God's Children"* Bible study, and ways to contact me with questions, comments, or more information.

If you would like for me to speak to your large or small group, you can contact me through this website for more information.

Additionally, under the Resources tab, you will find the current contact/source information for the Resources mentioned in this book. They include, but are not limited to:

http://www.ultimatesource.tv

http://www.Soulwork.org

http://www.beatcancer.org

Made in the USA
San Bernardino, CA
05 February 2018